The Art of
Inner Change

A Companion Guide

Carmen Beese & Gabriela Ribeiro

Copyright 2024 – The Art of Inner Change – A Companion Guide by Carmen Beese and Gabriela Ribeiro BSc (Hons) Psychology

All rights reserved. No part of this publication may be reproduced without explicit permission from the publisher.

Contents

Introduction: 7
Harvard Adult Development Study 13
Emotional Regulation 19
Gratitude 30
Awe 39
Escaping the Grip of the Victim Mindset 45
Relaxing Your Nervous System 52
Breath: Your Hidden Superpower 57
Journalling 63
Mindfulness: The Art of Being Present 71
From Plate to Peace 84
Embracing Self-Care 101
The Power of Play 114
Attachment Theory 120
The Grief Puzzle 134
Trauma: The Unseen Scars Within 140
Transgenerational Trauma 154
Epilogue 167
References & Resources: 169

Introduction:

In the quiet moments between our commitments and chaos, where the noise fades and the silence speaks, we find ourselves on the brink of introspection. It's here, in these fleeting, profound instances, that we realise how often we become strangers to ourselves, lost among the roles we play and the lives we lead. This book is your invitation to pause, to breathe, and to embark on the most significant journey you'll ever undertake — a journey into your complex, beautiful inner cosmos.

Our journey starts in the realm of our emotions, a place where we sometimes find ourselves struggling to manage the various feelings influencing our reactions and behaviour. This is where we learn about emotional regulation, the process of acknowledging our emotions and expressing them in a beneficial manner. It involves seeing our emotions as indicators of our state, not as absolute rulers, and realizing that we have the innate ability to handle our emotional challenges effectively.

As we move forward from understanding emotional regulation, we enter the impactful sphere of gratitude. This concept, though straightforward, has profound effects, enabling us to perceive our surroundings with a sense of thankfulness, and acknowledging value in aspects we might typically ignore. Gratitude enhances our perspective, making us realise that what we possess is sufficient, sometimes even abundant. It encourages us to recognise that life's beauty and richness don't solely reside in grand events but also in simple, everyday occurrences. This realisation is what adds an extraordinary layer to our ordinary lives.

As we progress, we step into the area of awe, an emotion often lost amidst our daily commotions. Reconnecting with awe requires us to see the world with fresh, curious eyes, much like a child, and to appreciate the expansive universe and the simple details without feeling overwhelmed. This journey helps us recognise that wonder is present everywhere, from the basic elements of nature to the complicated ties of human connections, all inviting a newfound appreciation.

Navigating through personal transformation, we often confront internal obstacles, particularly the victim mindset that can dominate our thoughts. Overcoming this challenge doesn't mean ignoring our difficulties; rather, it involves taking control of our own story. It's recognising that although we don't have power over everything that happens to us, we can choose how we interpret and respond to these events. This realisation is our key to freedom and the restoration of our personal autonomy.

In the relentless rush of our daily routines, we deeply crave moments of peace and solace. Exploring this subject reveals the science of calming our nervous system, allowing us to access a level of tranquillity that often seems unattainable. Through a blend of scientifically supported methods and ancient wisdom, we come to understand that true peace is not distant but present within us, ready to be embraced.

Breath, the subtle, often unnoticed rhythm of our existence, takes centre stage in our ongoing journey. This life force, so automatic yet so powerful, emerges as a tool of transformation. We dive into practices, old and new, realising that in the cadence of our breath lies the secret to health, vitality, and equanimity. This revelation isn't just scientific; it's almost spiritual.

Further along, we come to a clearing — a space for reflection and clarity, through the practice of journaling. It's here we learn that our pens hold power, that the act of pouring ourselves onto paper is not just cathartic; it's revelatory. It's a mirror that reflects our fears, hopes, dreams, and the truth we often whisper to ourselves. In writing, we engage in a sacred dialogue with our deepest selves.

As our path winds, we're introduced to the art of presence — mindfulness. In a world vying for our attention, being wholly present is a revolutionary act. It's a return to clarity, a pulling away from the distractions and the noise, and a kind invitation to ourselves to simply be. It's here we learn that life is available only in the present moment and that our anxiety, fears, and worries often stem from a departure from the 'now.'

Our exploration then takes a tangible turn, acknowledging the profound connection between our bodies and minds. We explore the world of nutrition, understanding that what we feed our bodies, we feed our souls. Our relationship with food is reframed, not as a mundane act of consumption but as an act of nourishment, self-respect, and even healing.

In the realm of self-care, we dismantle misconceptions, understanding that caring for ourselves is not indulgent but essential. It's an act of survival, a commitment we make to our well-being, ensuring we can show up as our best selves in every role we assume. It's a reminder that we, too, deserve the love, care, and respect we so freely give to others.

Yet, no journey is complete without its valleys. The path through grief is one we walk with heavy hearts, but it's here we learn the depth of our love, the strength of our spirit, and the resilience inherent in our humanity. It's a walk that teaches us empathy, compassion, and the heartrending beauty of our human experience.

As our expedition draws to a close, we face perhaps our most challenging terrain — trauma. These are the unseen, often unspoken scars that mark our inner landscapes, shaping our responses, fears, and even our dreams. Addressing these wounds is perhaps our most sacred work, demanding of us immense courage, compassion, and a deep commitment to our healing.

This book, your companion on this journey, is more than a guide. It's a testament to the human spirit, to our endless capacity for growth, healing, and transformation. It's an ode to the beauty, complexity, and incredible resilience of our beings. As you traverse these pages, know that you're undertaking the most sacred of journeys — the journey within.

So, dear readers, as you embark, remember that these words are not just passages in a book; they are signposts to your inner world. This journey is yours — through the valleys and over the mountains, through laughter and tears, through discoveries and healing. May you find within these pages not just information, but transformation. Welcome, to The Art of Inner Change – A Companion Guide.

Harvard Adult Development Study

I wanted to kickstart our conversation by sharing something really fascinating with you. Have you ever heard of the Harvard Adult Development Study?

Researchers have been keeping tabs on about 700 individuals for over 80 years – it's like watching a captivating movie that spans generations! They're not just observing these folks, but also their partners and children. It's like getting to know an entire interconnected community.

The participants were a diverse group. Two groups, in particular, were tracked:

Harvard Sophomores: These were college students who studied at Harvard. They came from relatively privileged backgrounds.

Disadvantaged Families: These individuals hailed from Boston's poorest neighbourhoods. They were adolescents at high risk for mental health issues.

The beauty of the study was in its diversity.

By choosing such varied participants, the researchers could gain insights into how different life circumstances affected overall well-being.

Now, here's the exciting part – all this detective work isn't just for entertainment; it's helping scientists unravel the mysteries of a fulfilling life. They're uncovering what truly leads to happiness, health, and success by studying the real, unscripted experiences of these people. It's like having a wise friend who's been through it all, sharing their secrets with us. So, as we embark on our journey with "The Art of Inner Change," let's tap into the invaluable lessons from this lifelong study to enrich our own lives!

Quality Relationships Are the True Fountain of Youth

Think of your relationships as magic potions that keep you young and healthy. This study found that people who have warm, close relationships with family and friends tend to be happier and live longer. Imagine these connections as shields, protecting you from the storms of life. So, remember, it's not about the quantity of friends, but the quality of those connections that truly matters.

Think about it this way: if you have five close friends who you can trust, confide in, and share your joys and sorrows with,

you're likely to experience greater happiness than if you have a hundred superficial relationships. Authentic, supportive relationships provide a buffer against life's inevitable challenges, helping you navigate rough waters with greater resilience.
Feeling lonely and isolated can harm one's health. The study found that people who felt lonely were more likely to experience physical decline and die younger.

One of the most heartwarming findings was that even in one's 80s, a change in the way one lived and perceived relationships could positively affect their health. It's never too late to forge new friendships or mend broken ties.

Your heart is like a playful puppy – it thrives when it's happy. The researchers discovered that folks who are content in their relationships experience lower stress levels and a healthier heart. It's like your heart doing a little dance of joy when you're surrounded by people who care about you.

Growing Old, Yet Staying Sharp

Think of your brain as a muscle – the more you exercise it, the stronger it gets. The study revealed that people who challenge their minds with new experiences and keep learning as they age are more likely to stay mentally sharp. Imagine your brain as a clever detective, always excited to solve new puzzles.

No Room for Regrets

Life is like a giant canvas, and you're the artist creating your masterpiece. The study found that people who hold onto regrets and negative emotions tend to have unhappier lives. It's like carrying around a bag of rocks that weighs you down. Let go of those regrets and allow your canvas to be filled with bright, joyful colours.

Weathering Storms with Resilience

Life is a rollercoaster, with its ups and downs. The study highlighted that being resilient – bouncing back from tough times – is crucial for a fulfilling life. Think of yourself as a tree in a storm; even if you bend, you won't break. Resilience helps you weather the storms of life without losing your leaves.

Love Your Body, Love Your Life

Taking care of your body matters! The study showed that maintaining good physical health through exercise, a balanced diet, and proper sleep can lead to a happier and longer life. Treat your body like a cherished friend, and it'll be right there with you on all your exciting escapades.

Give to Receive

The boomerang effect – what you throw out comes right back to you. The study found that people who give back through acts of kindness and volunteering tend to experience greater satisfaction and happiness. Planting seeds of joy leads to a beautiful garden of contentment.

Rolling with Change

To live is to be in constant state of flow and change. The study revealed that adapting to these changes is essential for well-being. Think of yourself as a skilled surfer riding the waves of change. Embracing new chapters with open arms can lead to a more exciting and fulfilling journey.

Money Isn't Everything, But Security Matters

Money is a tool in your toolbox, helping you build the life you want. The study showed that while money doesn't guarantee happiness, having financial stability and security can significantly impact your well-being. It's like having a sturdy umbrella in a rainstorm – it won't stop the rain, but it'll keep you dry.

Find Your Passion and Flourish

Your passions are stars guiding you through life's vast night sky. The study highlighted that engaging in activities that make your heart sing leads to a more fulfilling existence. Pursue your passions like a treasure hunt – each discovery adds a glimmer to your life's map.

From the initial group that embarked on this journey, a remarkable 19 remain, all in their mid-90s. The study's scope has expanded, now including over 1,300 of their descendants, who are currently in their 50s and 60s. Today, the total number of participants is approximately 1,319, and this number is set to increase as the study continues to enrol more descendants of the original members.

Over 100 participants have generously donated their brains for the greater good of research. These precious donations offer invaluable insights into understanding how our brains evolve with age, how our daily choices and societal interactions shape our neural pathways and the mysteries behind certain brain-related diseases. Additionally, researchers are granted access to detailed health records and life stories from the Harvard Study, creating a comprehensive picture that links individual life experiences with brain findings. This combined data provides a unique opportunity to further our understanding of the intricate workings of the human brain.

The Harvard Study of Adult Development paints a colourful picture of what it takes to live a fulfilling, joyful, and meaningful life. It's like a guidebook for crafting your own adventure – reminding you that meaningful relationships, a healthy mind and body, resilience, generosity, adaptability, financial security, and pursuing passions are the keys to unlocking a treasure trove of happiness.

So, as you navigate through life, remember these nuggets of wisdom from the Harvard Study: treasure your relationships, keep your heart and mind in tip-top shape, let go of regrets, bounce back with resilience, treat your body well, give without expecting, embrace change, find your passions, and understand that money has its place. With these insights, you'll be well-equipped to sail the seas of life with a big grin on your face and a heart full of happiness. Happy adventuring!

"If you do not manage your emotions, then your emotions will manage you.
　　　　　　　　　　　　~Dr. Les Greenberg~

Emotional Regulation

The Importance of Embracing Your Emotions and Mastering Mood Swings

Emotions are fundamental components that add depth, richness, and meaning to our lives. They are formed through our experiences and interactions, creating a complex and dynamic range of feelings. In life, it is crucial to experience and acknowledge these emotions, encompassing both positive and negative aspects. Let's explore the significance of fully experiencing your emotions, comprehending the changes in moods, and mastering the skill of emotional regulation.

Embracing Your Emotions: Unveiling the Canvas of Your Inner World

Your emotions form a diverse and complex spectrum, each contributing uniquely to your personal experience. They range from the joy and brightness of happiness to the profound and often challenging depths of sadness. Every emotion has a role in shaping and narrating your life's story.

Recent research highlights the benefits of embracing your emotions. A study by Stanford University revealed that acknowledging and naming your emotions can lessen their impact. This process of recognition helps in understanding that these emotional states are natural and manageable, rather than overwhelming. Such emotional awareness is crucial for improved mental health and an enhanced sense of overall well-being.

Understanding Mood Fluctuations: Accepting Low Emotional Periods

Our moods naturally vary, similar to the inevitable changes in day-to-day weather. There are times when we might feel a bit gloomy, with cheerfulness seeming to retreat. Such feelings are a normal part of life. It's important to recognise that feeling negative emotions doesn't signify weakness or inadequacy. Instead, these moments of feeling down are a crucial aspect of our human journey, contributing to our growth and emotional resilience.

Your emotions can exhibit a wide range of intensity and pace, not unlike the varying currents of a river. There are moments when they may feel intense and full of energy, and other times when they become more subdued and calmer. These mood changes are not defining characteristics of who you are, but rather reflections of the dynamic and ever-changing nature of our lives and experiences.

The Timely Tide: How Long You Stay with an Emotion Matters

Just as the tide eventually recedes, emotions also have a natural ebb and flow. It's not about avoiding negative emotions but understanding that they don't have to become permanent residents in your emotional landscape. The key is to recognise when a temporary feeling begins to linger longer than it should.

Consider your emotions as guests at a party. While some are welcome to stay for a while, others might overstay their welcome. It's okay to kindly usher out the emotions that are overstaying their time, allowing room for fresher and more positive feelings to take their place.

A study published in the "Journal of Personality and Social Psychology" highlights the importance of emotional processing. It found that people who engaged in actively processing and understanding their emotions experienced greater psychological well-being over time.

Life is filled with a wide array of emotions, each contributing to a diverse and fulfilling existence. Embracing every emotion, from joy to sadness, is vital for a rich life. It's important to acknowledge that, like any natural process, our moods fluctuate. Experiencing days when you feel low is normal and part of life's rhythm. The key lies in how you manage and respond to these changes.

Emotional regulation is the process that helps you manage and balance your feelings. It involves caring for and attending to your emotions appropriately. Allowing your emotions to be felt and expressed is crucial, but it's also important to prevent them from dominating your life excessively. Studies highlight the benefits of being aware of and effectively regulating your emotions, which is a significant step towards improved overall well-being.

How Emotions Can Hook Us

Dr. Candace Pert is a pioneering neuroscientist and pharmacologist, her theory delves into the intricate interplay between emotions and the body, proposing that emotions are not just mental states, but also involve a biochemical component that can lead to emotional addiction.

According to her theory, neuropeptides act as messengers, bridging the gap between the mind and the body, transmitting emotional information. Pert suggests that when we experience certain emotions, the corresponding neuropeptides are released, creating a biochemical response that can be pleasurable and even addictive.

Just as individuals can develop dependencies on substances, Dr. Pert's theory posits that repeated exposure to specific emotions can lead to a pattern of seeking out situations and experiences that trigger the release of those neuropeptides.

This emotional addiction, she suggests, can profoundly impact our behaviour, decision-making processes, relationships, and even our overall well-being, underscoring the intricate connection between our emotional experiences and the biochemical processes within our bodies.

So, the next time you experience an emotion, welcome and accept it as part of your life. Understand that it is a component of your story, but not its entirety. Your emotional experiences are continuously evolving, and you have the ability to shape and understand them.

Mastering the Art of Emotional Regulation: Navigating the Storms

Just as a skilled sailor navigates through rough waters, emotional regulation empowers us to navigate the storms of emotions with grace and resilience. This skill doesn't mean suppressing emotions or pretending they don't exist. Instead, it's about acknowledging, understanding, and managing them effectively.

Think of your emotions as a garden. Just as you tend to your plants by providing water, sunlight, and care, you can tend to your emotions by giving them attention, validation, and understanding. When you experience a surge of anger or sadness, take a moment to observe it without judgment. This practice creates a safe space for your emotions to express themselves.

Research published in the journal "Psychological Science" suggests that practicing emotional regulation can lead to improved psychological well-being and better interpersonal relationships. This is akin to nurturing your garden, where the more attention you give, the more vibrant and flourishing it becomes.

Here are some tips on how to ride the roller coaster of emotions with finesse. Let's dive into some practical ways to become an emotional ninja, backed by science!

1. Label Your Emotions:
Identifying and naming your emotions is a crucial step in understanding yourself. When you recognise and verbalise what you're feeling, it helps your brain to start processing and managing these emotions. For example, if you're feeling upset or irritated, acknowledging it by saying, "I'm feeling frustrated right now" can be beneficial.

Brené Brown, a well-known research professor and author, has contributed significantly to psychology and personal development, especially in the area of identifying emotions. Since 2006, Brown and her team have been exploring how people identify and articulate their emotions.

Interestingly, they found that many people typically identify only a limited range of emotions, commonly categorised as 'Bad,' 'Sad,' and 'Glad.' 'Bad' encompasses general negative feelings, 'Sad' relates to feelings of sorrow and loss, and 'Glad' corresponds to positive, happy emotions.

However, this limited range is like having a very basic set of tools to understand a wide and varied emotional experience. The reality is, our emotional spectrum is much broader and more nuanced than just these three categories.

By learning to name a wider range of emotions, we essentially expand our emotional understanding. This enhanced vocabulary allows for more precise expression and better comprehension of our own feelings and those of others.

One of the key ideas from Brown's work is that by naming our emotions, we gain more control over them. Instead of being overwhelmed by or suppressing our feelings, we can confront and analyse them more effectively.

Here's why this is important:
Increased Self-Awareness: When we name our emotions, we gain a clearer understanding of what we are feeling. Emotions can often be complex and intertwined, making it challenging to pinpoint their source. By giving emotions names such as "disappointed" instead of just sad or "lonely" instead of just sad we can distinguish between them and better comprehend their origins.

Emotional Regulation: Naming emotions is a fundamental step in emotional regulation. Once we recognise what we're feeling, we can choose how to respond to those emotions. This awareness allows us to make more conscious decisions about how we express ourselves, which can lead to healthier interactions with others.

Effective Communication: Accurate emotional labelling facilitates communication with others. When we can clearly express our emotions, we enable those around us to understand our needs, perspectives, and boundaries. This fosters better interpersonal relationships and reduces misunderstandings.

Empathy and Connection: Brown also emphasises the role of naming emotions in building empathy. When we can identify and understand our own emotions, we become better equipped to empathise with other people's emotional experiences. This, in turn, enhances our ability to connect on a deeper, more authentic level.

Reduced Shame and Vulnerability: Naming emotions helps to reduce the shame and vulnerability that often accompany them. Instead of feeling weak or flawed for experiencing certain emotions, we acknowledge that emotions are a natural part of being human. This recognition can lead to greater self-acceptance and self-compassion.

Brown encourages the use of specific emotion words rather than generic labels. For example, instead of merely saying "I feel bad," one might say, "I feel disappointed" or "I feel hurt." This precision in emotional language not only clarifies our own experiences but also invites others to engage in more meaningful conversations about feelings.

According to Brené Brown, naming emotions is a powerful tool for emotional intelligence and personal growth. It allows us to navigate the complexities of our inner world, communicate effectively with others, and build deeper, more meaningful connections. By embracing this practice, we can become more emotionally resilient and better equipped to face life's challenges with empathy and authenticity.

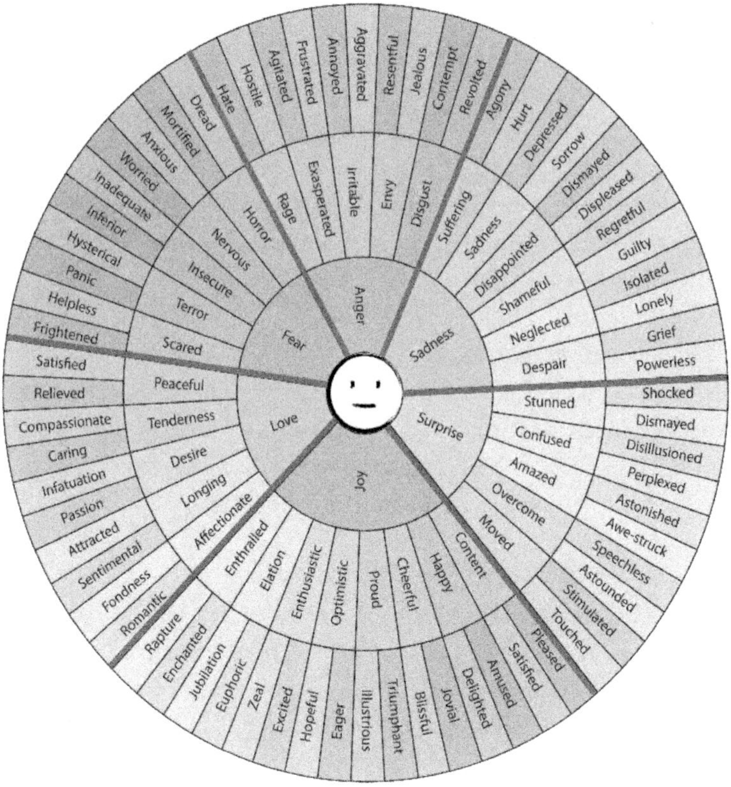
Anger
Sadness
Surprise
Joy
Love
Fear
Rage
Exasperated
Irritable
Envy
Disgust
Suffering
Sadness
Disappointed
Shameful
Neglected
Despair
Stunned
Confused
Amazed
Overcome
Moved
Content
Happy
Cheerful
Proud
Optimistic
Enthusiastic
Elation
Enthralled
Affectionate
Longing
Desire
Tenderness
Peaceful
Scared
Terror
Insecure
Nervous
Horror
Hate
Hostile
Agitated
Frustrated
Annoyed
Aggravated
Resentful
Jealous
Contempt
Revolted
Agony
Hurt
Depressed
Sorrow
Dismayed
Displeased
Regretful
Guilty
Isolated
Lonely
Grief
Powerless
Shocked
Dismayed
Disillusioned
Perplexed
Astonished
Awe-struck
Speechless
Astounded
Stimulated
Touched
Pleased
Satisfied
Amused
Delighted
Jovial
Blissful
Triumphant
Illustrious
Eager
Hopeful
Excited
Zeal
Euphoric
Jubilation
Enchanted
Rapture
Romantic
Fondness
Sentimental
Attracted
Passion
Infatuation
Caring
Compassionate
Relieved
Satisfied
Frightened
Helpless
Panic
Hysterical
Inferior
Inadequate
Worried
Anxious
Mortified
Dread

2. Take a Breath:
When you're feeling overwhelmed by emotions, take a moment to breathe deeply. Deep breathing is more than just a way to stay alive; it's a helpful tool to calm your emotions. Breathing deeply tells your brain to relax, helping you think more clearly. Studies have shown that deep breathing reduces stress and anxiety, making you feel more grounded.

3. Find Your Happy Distraction:
Doing something you enjoy, like listening to music, reading, or drawing, can change your mood for the better. Research suggests that engaging in enjoyable activities can lift your spirits and help you handle difficult emotions.

4. The Power of Pause:
When you start feeling a strong emotion, take a short break. Pausing gives you time to think before you react, which can lead to better decisions. This is supported by research that highlights the benefits of taking a moment to reflect.

5. Talk it Out:
Talking about your emotions with someone you trust can really help. It's like sharing a problem and making it lighter. Conversations with friends, family, or a therapist can reduce stress and offer new perspectives.

6. Write It Down:
Writing about your feelings in a journal can help you understand them better. Studies show that journaling improves emotional health and can even strengthen your immune system. So, grab a pen and start expressing your feelings on paper!

7. Mindfulness Magic:
Practicing mindfulness helps you focus on the present and not get overwhelmed by your emotions. Research has shown that mindfulness improves your ability to manage emotions and reduces negativity.

8. Practice, Practice, Practice:
Getting better at managing your emotions takes regular practice, just like improving in a sport. The more you use these techniques, the better you'll become at handling your feelings.

9. Be Kind to Yourself:
Treat yourself with kindness and compassion, especially during tough times. Studies show that being self-compassionate is important in dealing with emotions. Remember, you're doing your best, and that's enough!

10. Seek Professional Help:
If you're struggling with your emotions and can't seem to find a way out, consider talking to a professional. Therapists can provide valuable guidance, just like doctors do for physical health. Therapy has been proven to significantly improve emotional well-being.

Remember, dealing with emotions is a journey, and you're not alone. With patience and practice, you can learn to manage your feelings effectively. Your emotional health is worth the effort, and with time, you'll get better at understanding and regulating your emotions!

> "Gratitude unlocks the fullness of life. It turns what we have into enough, and more. It turns denial into acceptance, chaos to order, confusion to clarity. It can turn a meal into a feast, a house into a home, a stranger into a friend."
>
> ~Melody Beattie~

Gratitude

The Power of Gratitude: A Path to Well-being and Happiness

In our everyday lives, there's something really special we can do to make ourselves feel happier – it's called expressing gratitude. It's like a magic trick that science and people all over the world have discovered. Expressing gratitude can do amazing things for how we feel and how happy we are. Scientists have studied it, and even people from way back in time thought it was a great idea. So, if you want to have a better and more enjoyable life, expressing gratitude is the way to go!

The Science of Gratitude: A Robust Foundation

Think of gratitude like really good soil, the kind that helps positive feelings and mental strength grow inside us. Scientists have done a lot of research on gratitude, and it's become a big thing in the science world. They've looked at how it affects our feelings, our bodies, and even how we get along with other people. All this research is like a big library of knowledge, and it shows us that gratitude isn't just a passing feeling – it can actually change our lives.

Lots of studies have found that when we practice gratitude, it makes us feel better and happier. I decided to count the studies on Gratitude! – I was on a roll I got to 510 and then I realised there's a whole galaxy out there. We just can't contest the countless studies on gratitude.

For instance, a study published in the journal "Psychological Science" revealed that participants who engaged in gratitude exercises reported higher levels of life satisfaction and positive emotions compared to those who didn't. A meta-analysis conducted by David R. Cregg and Jennifer S. Cheavens and published in the Journal of Happiness Studies found that individuals who kept gratitude journals experienced reduced symptoms of depression and anxiety.

Even more intriguingly, gratitude appears to have a tangible impact on our brains. Neuroscientists have investigated the neurological underpinnings of gratitude, discovering that expressing gratitude activates brain regions associated with reward, empathy, and emotional processing. This neurological dance creates a positive feedback loop, enhancing our ability to experience and express gratitude, further amplifying its benefits.

Unpacking the Benefits of Gratitude

Gratitude is like a multifaceted gem, each facet representing a unique benefit that contributes to our overall well-being. Let's uncover some of these dazzling facets:

Enhanced Mental Health:
Gratitude acts as a shield against negative emotions. When we focus on what we're thankful for, it becomes harder for stress and anxiety to take root. In fact, a study published in the "Journal of Happiness Studies" found that practicing gratitude was associated with a significant reduction in symptoms of post-traumatic stress disorder (PTSD).

Improved Relationships:
Just as sunlight nourishes plants, gratitude nurtures relationships. Expressing gratitude fosters connection, deepens bonds, and enhances social interactions. Research published in the "Journal of Personality and Social Psychology" showed that people who express gratitude towards their partners experience more relationship satisfaction and are more likely to stay committed.

Physical Well-being:
Gratitude isn't confined to the realm of the mind; it extends its benevolent touch to our physical health. A study published in "Personality and Individual Differences" revealed that individuals who practiced gratitude had lower blood pressure and improved heart health.

Resilience and Coping:
Harnessing the power of gratitude is more than just a feel-good activity; it's a proven strategy for enhancing your psychological strength. Intriguing findings published in 'Personality and

Individual Differences' reveal that regular gratitude practice can significantly boost your mental toughness. This means that by simply recognising and appreciating the positives in your life, you're effectively building a stronger, more resilient mindset, ready to face life's ups and downs with a more balanced perspective.

Better Sleep:
If you're looking for a natural way to improve your sleep, consider the practice of gratitude. Research, including a notable study from 'Applied Psychology: Health and Well-Being,' has discovered that the simple act of writing down things you're grateful for before bedtime can lead to improved sleep quality. This practice seems to have a calming effect on the mind, helping to reduce intrusive thoughts and pave the way for a more restful and rejuvenating night's sleep.

Increased Empathy:
Gratitude opens our eyes to the goodness around us, fostering empathy and compassion. A study published in "Emotion" showed that individuals who experienced gratitude were more likely to display prosocial behaviours, indicating a heightened sense of empathy.

Cultivating Gratitude: A Practice for All

Understanding the importance of gratitude in our lives is just the first step; the next is integrating it into our daily routines. Cultivating gratitude can be simple yet impactful, and here are some easy ways to do it:

Gratitude Journaling:
Keeping a gratitude journal is a straightforward and powerful method. Each day, take a few moments to write down things you're grateful for. These could be small joys, like the comfort of your favourite chair, the taste of a good meal, or larger aspects of your life like supportive friends and family. The act of writing them down can help you focus on the positive aspects of your life, reinforcing a sense of contentment and appreciation.

Mindful Moments:
Incorporate gratitude into your daily life by taking brief pauses to acknowledge the good around you. This could be as simple as appreciating a quiet moment during a busy day, the warmth of the sun on your skin, or a kind gesture from a stranger. By acknowledging these moments, you train your mind to notice and appreciate the positive, however small it might seem.

Gratitude Letters:
Writing gratitude letters is a meaningful way to express your appreciation for others. Take some time to write a letter to someone who has made a difference in your life, thanking them for their impact. You don't necessarily have to send the letter; the act of writing it can be a fulfilling experience in itself, helping you recognise and value the positive relationships in your life.

Three Good Things:
Envision gratitude as a daily ritual. Before you sleep, identify three things that went well during the day and why they made you feel grateful. This practice shifts your focus from what went wrong to what went right.

Incorporating Gratitude into Daily Life: Creative Ideas

Gratitude Jar:
Set up a jar in a common area of your home. Each day, write down something you're grateful for on a small piece of paper and drop it into the jar. This could be anything from a kind gesture someone made to something good that happened that day. Over time, you'll see the jar fill up, creating a visual representation of all the positive things in your life.

Gratitude Walks:
Turn your regular walks into an opportunity for gratitude. As you walk, make a conscious effort to observe and appreciate the beauty around you. Notice the colors of the sky, the patterns of the leaves, or the sounds of the city or nature. Let this awareness bring a sense of thankfulness for the world you're a part of.

Mealtime Gratitude:
Before you start eating, pause for a moment to express gratitude for your meal. Think about the effort that went into preparing it and the sources of the ingredients. This practice can help you appreciate the food more and can also be a gentle reminder to eat mindfully.

Gratitude Collage:
Create a collage that represents the things you're thankful for. Collect pictures, inspirational quotes, or items that remind you of happy moments. Arrange them on a board or in a scrapbook. This visual collection can serve as a source of comfort and positivity whenever you need it.

Let's celebrate the meaningful and tangible aspects of life that often go unnoticed. Here's a list of things to be grateful for that remind us of the richness of our existence:

Waking Up in a Comfortable Bed
Roof Over My Head
Clean Water
Food on the Table
Warm Clothing
Access to Education
Supportive Friends and Family
Stable Income
Reliable Transportation
Access to Healthcare
Freedom and Safety
Our planet
Nature
Sunrises
Sunsets

In the broad spectrum of human experiences, gratitude emerges as a source of strength and resilience. Like a skill that needs care and attention, practicing gratitude can be integrated effortlessly into our lives, brightening our days with feelings of contentment, joy, and well-being.

As countless studies and research attest, the benefits of gratitude are far from mere speculation. Like a foundation built upon solid rock, the science behind gratitude provides a robust base for its claims. Through gratitude, we tap into a wellspring of positivity that transcends cultures, generations, and individual circumstances. It's a practice that reminds us to turn our focus towards the blessings that grace our lives, cultivating an attitude of gratitude that warms our hearts and lights our paths.

What are you truly grateful for?

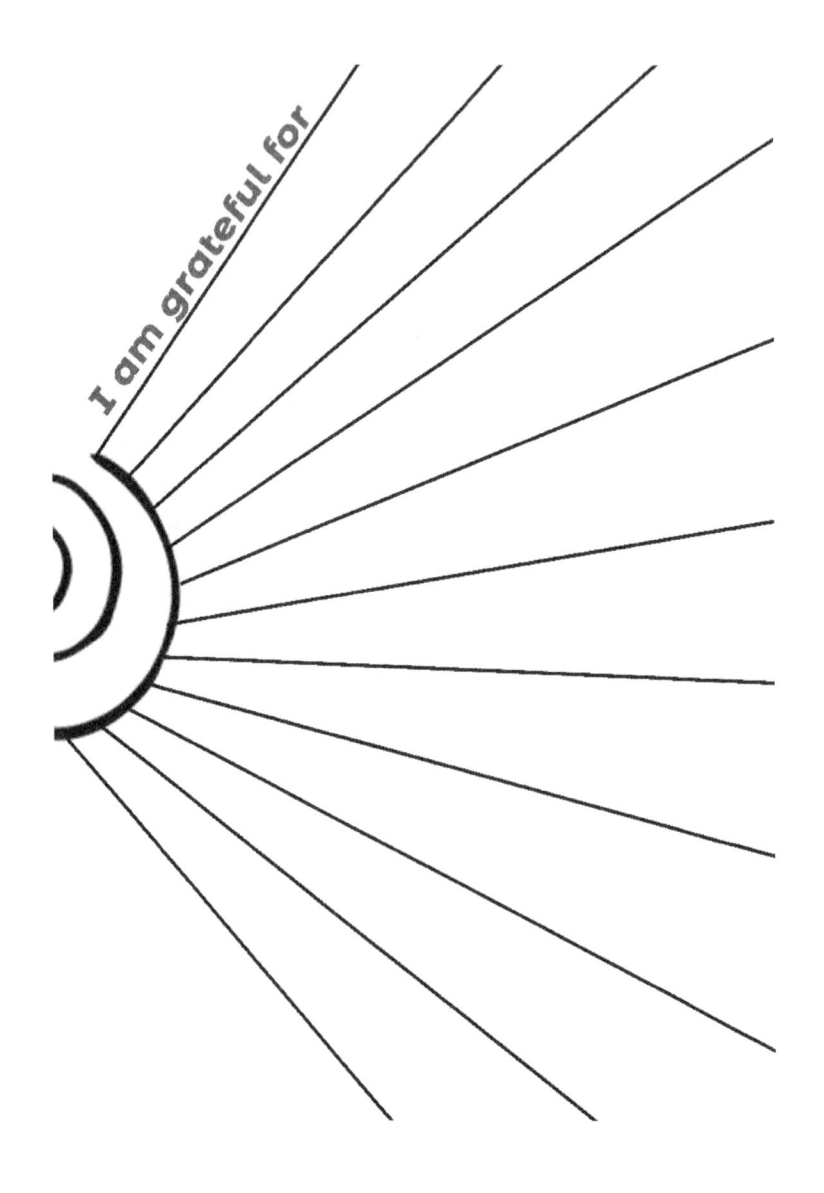

I am grateful for

"Awe is the feeling of being in the presence of something vast that transcends your understanding of the world."
~Dacher Keltner~

Awe

Have you ever felt deeply moved and overwhelmed by the magnificence of something, so much so that you were left speechless? This intense feeling, often causing goosebumps and a sense of grandeur, is what Professor Dacher Keltner has been passionately exploring. He delves into the science behind this emotion, commonly known as awe.

Professor Keltner's research opens up a fascinating area of human emotion. He investigates how experiencing awe can profoundly impact our lives. It's all about those moments that make us feel small in the face of something much larger than ourselves, yet connected in a profound way to the world and people around us.

Let's take a journey into the captivating world of awe and learn about the incredible work of Professor Keltner.

Professor Dacher Keltner is a friendly and inquisitive individual brimming with contagious enthusiasm for unravelling the complex emotions that influence our lives. He's not your average researcher; he holds the position of a psychology professor at the University of California, Berkeley and is a pioneer in the field of emotions. His expertise extends to the realm of awe, where he's one of the foremost authorities, and his research has significantly contributed to our understanding of its numerous advantages. Throughout his career, Professor Keltner has devoted himself to exploring human emotions, with a special focus on the captivating world of awe.

What exactly is awe? Think about a breathtaking sunset that leaves you marvelling at the beauty of nature, or standing in the shadow of a towering mountain that fills you with a sense of insignificance and wonder. That feeling—that's awe. It's that overwhelming emotion that arises when we encounter something larger than ourselves, something that challenges our understanding of the world.

Professor Keltner, along with his team, has been on a quest to unravel the science behind awe. They've discovered that awe isn't just a fleeting emotion; it has a profound impact on our well-being. When we experience awe, we're not just passive observers. Our brains light up with activity, and our bodies respond too. It's like a symphony of awe where every part of our being joins in the melody.

Now, you might be wondering, why should we care about awe? Professor Dacher Keltner's research uncovers something extraordinary about awe: it can alter our perception of time. When we experience moments of awe, time seems to expand, allowing us to deeply immerse ourselves and savour these instances more fully. This unique effect of awe makes our most memorable experiences feel even richer and more enduring, offering a sense of having more time to appreciate life's wonders.

But that's not all. Awe also has the incredible ability to make us feel more connected to others. Imagine awe as a bridge that connects hearts. When we experience awe together, whether it's watching a mesmerising performance or witnessing a natural wonder, we feel a sense of unity with those around us. It's as if we're all in this grand adventure called life together.

Alright, so awe sounds pretty awesome, but how does it impact our overall well-being? Professor Keltner and his colleagues have found that experiencing awe can actually boost our happiness. When we're caught up in the vastness of the universe or the intricacies of a piece of art, our own worries and stresses seem to take a back seat. It's like awe sweeps away the mental clutter, making room for joy and contentment.

But there's even more to the story. Awe might just be the superhero we need for our health. Studies have suggested that regularly experiencing awe can lead to lower levels of inflammation in our bodies. It's like awe has this magical ability to calm down the storms within us, promoting better health and well-being.

Keltner and his colleagues have conducted a number of studies on the effects of awe. One study found that people who experienced awe were more likely to help others, even when it was costly to do so.

Worksheet:

1. Describe a time when you felt a sense of awe. What triggered it? How did it make you feel about yourself and the world around you?

   _____
   _____
   _____
   _____
   _____
   _____

2. How does experiencing awe affect your perception of your problems or concerns? How might it shift your perspective on personal issues or stresses?

   _____
   _____
   _____
   _____
   _____
   _____

3. Set some long-term goals to incorporate awe into your life more regularly. How will you seek out new awe-inspiring experiences?

   _____
   _____
   _____
   _____
   _____
   _____

> *"No one can make you a victim but you. We can't control what happens to us, but we can control how we respond to it."*
>
> ~Dr. Edith Eger~

Escaping the Grip of the Victim Mindset

Imagine a world where every setback is seen as an opportunity, where challenges are embraced as chances to grow, and where every individual believes in their ability to shape their own destiny. This sounds like an idealistic dream, but it's within reach if we can break free from the shackles of the victim mindset. The victim mindset, a psychological phenomenon where individuals perceive themselves as helpless and blame external factors for their misfortunes, can have a profound impact on our lives and achievements. It's a subject that has attracted attention from various perspectives, including that of the former First Lady of the United States, Michelle Obama.

The Prison of Victimhood

The victim mindset is a cognitive trap that can hinder personal growth and success. When we fall into this mindset, we view ourselves as mere recipients of life's circumstances, trapped in a web of external forces beyond our control. This outlook can be crippling, preventing us from taking responsibility for our actions and choices. Instead of seeking solutions, we find comfort in assigning blame to others or the environment. This cycle keeps us from pursuing our goals and aspirations, as we see the odds as insurmountable and ourselves as powerless.

Michelle Obama, known for her inspirational speeches and empowering messages, has shared her thoughts on the victim mindset. She emphasises the importance of acknowledging challenges while also recognising one's agency to overcome them. In her memoir, "Becoming," she discusses her upbringing in a working-class neighbourhood, highlighting that although the odds were against her in many ways, she refused to adopt the victim mentality. She recognised that her circumstances didn't define her, and she made conscious choices to pursue education, personal growth, and eventually become the First Lady of the United States.

Mrs. Obama's viewpoint aligns with the idea that while external factors can present obstacles, our response to those obstacles holds the key to our success. By focusing on what we can control and taking proactive steps, we can rewrite our narrative and shatter the confines of the victim mindset.

Research Insights

Various studies in psychology and neuroscience shed light on the effects of the victim mindset on our lives and achievements. One notable study conducted by researchers at the University of Queensland in Australia explored the link between mindset and academic performance. The study found that students who exhibited a victim mentality were more likely to experience lower academic achievement. This was attributed to their tendency to attribute failure to external factors such as unfair grading, rather than recognising their role in studying effectively.

Another study, published in the "Journal of Personality and Social Psychology," delved into the impact of victim mentality on interpersonal relationships. The researchers found that individuals with a strong victim mindset tended to have poorer relationship quality, as they were more likely to blame their partners for conflicts and less likely to take responsibility for their contribution to the issues at hand.

Neuroscientific research also provides insights into how the victim mindset affects the brain. A study conducted at the University of Southern California used functional magnetic resonance imaging (fMRI) to observe brain activity in response to setbacks. The researchers found that individuals with a victim mindset exhibited heightened activity in brain regions associated with negative emotions and reduced activity in areas linked to problem-solving and resilience. This suggests that the victim mindset not only influences behaviour but also has a tangible impact on neural processes.

Breaking Free from the Victim Mindset

Escaping the grip of the victim mindset is undoubtedly challenging, but it is far from impossible. It requires a conscious effort to shift our perspective and take ownership of our lives. Here are some steps to consider:

1. Self-Awareness: Recognise when you're slipping into a victim mindset. Are you attributing your failures solely to external factors? Are you focusing on what you can't control rather than what you can?

2. Responsibility: Take ownership of your choices and actions. While circumstances may influence us, our responses are still under our control. Instead of blaming others, explore how you can adapt and grow.

3. Positive Framing: Reframe challenges as opportunities for growth. Instead of seeing setbacks as proof of your helplessness, view them as chances to learn and improve.

4. Empowerment: Embrace the idea that you have the power to shape your life. Set goals and take steps to achieve them, even if progress is incremental.

5. Mindfulness: Practice mindfulness to stay present and focused on the present moment. This can help you avoid dwelling on past misfortunes or worrying excessively about the future. More about this later.

6. Gratitude: Cultivate a sense of gratitude for the positive aspects of your life. Focusing on what you have can counteract the tendency to feel victimised by what you lack.

7. Seek Support: Surround yourself with people who uplift and encourage you. Seek out mentors, friends, or support groups that promote a positive outlook and personal growth.

The Transformational Journey

Breaking free from the victim mindset is not an overnight process. It's a journey that requires consistent effort and self-reflection. Remember that no one is immune to moments of self-doubt or challenges, but our response to these moments is what truly matters. By adopting an empowered mindset, you can reshape your life's trajectory and achieve the success you deserve.

In the words of Michelle Obama, "We need to do a better job of putting ourselves higher on our own 'to do' list." This sentiment encapsulates the essence of escaping the victim mindset. When we prioritise our own agency and growth, we unleash our potential to create a life filled with accomplishments, resilience, and fulfilment. So, why settle for the limitations of victimhood when the power to transform lies within us?

Self-Test: Assessing Victim Mindset

Instructions: Answer the following questions honestly with a "Yes" or "No." These questions are designed to help you self-assess whether you might have tendencies toward a victim mindset. Remember, this is for your personal insight and growth.

Questions	y	n
When things go wrong, do I often find myself blaming others instead of looking at my own role in the situation?		
Do I feel like bad things happen to me more than others, and that I have little to no control over these events?		
When faced with a problem, do I tend to give up easily, feeling like there's nothing I can do to change the situation?		
Do I often feel that life is unfair to me specifically, more than to others around me?		
Do I feel powerless or helpless when facing challenges, believing that I cannot make a positive change in my circumstances?		
Do I hold onto grudges or resentments toward others for my current problems or unhappiness?		
Do I feel unrecognised for my efforts and believe that others consistently overlook or undervalue me?		
Am I resistant to change or advice, feeling like nothing will make a difference in my situation?		
Do I struggle to take personal responsibility for my actions or the outcomes of my actions, preferring to attribute them to external factors?		
Do I spend more time complaining about a problem than actively seeking solutions or ways to overcome it?		

Scoring:

0-2 "Yes" Answers
You likely have a healthy perspective on life's challenges and a strong sense of personal agency.

3-5 "Yes" Answers
You may occasionally fall into victim-thinking patterns; awareness and proactive change can improve this.

6+ "Yes" Answers
You might have a tendency toward a victim mindset, which could be impacting your quality of life and relationships. Consider exploring this further with self-help resources or professional guidance.

"The nervous system can become a powerful ally in calming the mind and easing the body, given the right environment and attention."
~Dr. Jon Kabat-Zinn~

Relaxing Your Nervous System

Science-Backed Methods for Instant Calm

In today's chaotic world, stress and anxiety are always lurking around the corner. They can sneak up on us when we least expect it, leaving us feeling overwhelmed and exhausted. But there is good news! Science has discovered some amazing ways to quickly calm our nervous system and restore our sense of peace.

Let's dive into three of these methods that can help you achieve instant calm: the Physiological Sigh, the Butterfly Hug Variation, and Bilateral Eye Movement. So next time you're feeling stressed or anxious, try one of these methods. You may be surprised at how quickly they can help you feel better.

Method 1: The Physiological Sigh - A Breath of Relief

Imagine being able to reduce stress within seconds with a simple sigh. It sounds almost too good to be true, but science has shown that the physiological sigh is a natural mechanism our body employs to help us relax. How does it work? Well, let's break it down.

When you inhale twice, as in the physiological sigh, a fascinating chain reaction occurs within your body. The alveoli, those tiny air sacs in your lungs responsible for oxygen exchange, get a much-needed boost. These alveoli tend to collapse a bit during shallow breathing, which often accompanies stress. However, the double inhale of the sigh helps them re-inflate with air. This action increases the surface area of your lungs, leading to the more efficient removal of carbon dioxide (CO_2) from your body. And here's the kicker – efficient CO_2 removal signals to your body that it's safe to relax. As CO_2 levels drop, your body's fight-or-flight response takes a back seat, and a calm sensation sets in.

But that's not all! The second part of the physiological sigh involves a long exhale. When you exhale for a longer duration, it causes a gentle rise in pressure on the receptors within your heart. These receptors then send signals to your brain, coaxing it to slow down your heart rate. This reduction in heart rate contributes to the overall feeling of relaxation. It's like your body's very own relaxation prescription!

How to Do It:

1. Find a comfortable and quiet space.
2. Inhale gently and deeply through your nose.
3. Exhale slowly and completely through your mouth, making sure the exhale is longer than the inhale.
4. Repeat this process for a few cycles, focusing on the sensation of calmness with each exhale.

Method 2: Butterfly Hug Variation - Embrace Your Calm

Bilateral stimulation is a fancy term for a technique that engages both sides of your body or brain, often leading to relaxation and reduced anxiety. The Butterfly Hug Variation is a delightful twist on this concept that not only offers relaxation but also brings you into the present moment.

Much like bilateral eye movement, this method involves rhythmic and controlled movements. The unique aspect of the Butterfly Hug Variation is that it combines these movements with deep breaths, enhancing the sense of expansiveness and presence. This technique helps synchronise both hemispheres of your brain, creating a state of balance that promotes relaxation.

How to Do It:

1. Cross your arms over your chest, with your hands resting on your upper arms, resembling a self-hug.
2. Gently tap your hands on your upper arms alternately, creating a rhythmic motion. You can tap with a light pressure that feels comfortable.

3. As you tap, take slow and deep breaths, focusing on the rise and fall of your chest.
4. Engage in this rhythmic tapping and breathing for a few minutes, allowing yourself to be fully present in the moment.

Method 3: Bilateral Eye Movement - Swiftly Soothe Your Mind

Have you ever noticed how moving your eyes from side to side can have a calming effect? Science has explored this phenomenon and found that bilateral stimulation, such as eye movements, can significantly reduce fear and anxiety. This technique is a cornerstone of Eye Movement Desensitisation and Reprocessing (EMDR), a therapy known for its effectiveness in treating trauma and anxiety.

Bilateral eye movement works its magic by boosting brain activity in a way that diminishes fear responses. This method has been found to induce relaxation, enhance attentional flexibility (the ability to shift focus), create emotional distance from distressing thoughts, and reduce excessive worrying.

How to Do It:

1. Sit in a comfortable position and choose a focal point in front of you.
2. While keeping your head still, move your eyes slowly from side to side, as if you're watching a pendulum swing.
3. Take deep breaths as you continue this eye movement, allowing your mind to focus on the rhythmic motion.
4. Engage in this exercise for a few minutes, letting go of tension and stress with each eye movement.

These three methods offer fascinating insights into how our bodies and minds can be rapidly calmed through simple techniques. The Physiological Sigh leverages the power of breath to stimulate relaxation responses within our lungs and heart. The Butterfly Hug Variation adds a touch of physicality to bilateral stimulation, enhancing presence and grounding. Lastly, Bilateral Eye Movement taps into the brain's natural capacity to reduce fear and anxiety, providing a quick pathway to relaxation.

Next time stress comes knocking, remember these scientifically backed methods that can whisk you away from tension and anxiety in a matter of moments. Embrace the power of your breath, the magic of rhythmic movements, and the soothing influence of your eyes, and let relaxation become your superpower in the hustle and bustle of life.

> *"Breath is the bridge which connects life to consciousness, which unites your body to your thoughts."*
>
> ~Thich Nhat Hanh~

Breath: Your Hidden Superpower

Breathing is a basic part of our lives that we often don't pay much attention to. Daniel Lieberman and James Nestor, experts in this field, explain why it's important to breathe correctly. They discuss how mouth breathing can be harmful and highlight the benefits of proper breathing. They share insights into how effective breathing can positively impact our health and well-being.

Lieberman, an evolutionary biologist, explains that our ancestors needed good breathing techniques for their survival and physical activities. He suggests that their ability to breathe well played a significant role in their endurance and mental alertness. Learning from these ancient breathing methods can help us improve our health today. This look into breathing teaches us about its important role in our overall well-being and how we can improve it.

Mastering the Diaphragm
Find your zen spot. Sit or lie down. Hand on chest, the other on the belly. Breathe in through your nose, feel your belly rise. Exhale, feel it fall. It's like filling and emptying a balloon. Do this daily and feel the difference.

The Nose Knows
Breathing through the nose isn't just for sniffing roses. Think of your nose as a high-tech air purifier. It fine-tunes the air, making it just right for your lungs. It's nature's way of ensuring every breath is gold standard.

The Art of Slow Breathing
Consider a peaceful stream next to a wild waterfall. Your breath can mimic that stream—calm and peaceful. James Nestor, in his outstanding work "Breath," underscores the beauty of relaxed breathing. Rapid, shallow breaths? They resemble turbulent waterfalls, causing agitation within our bodies. Yet, slow, purposeful breaths? They bring absolute serenity.

Breathing with Intent
Your breath is a vital part of your life, yet it's easy to overlook. Experts like Lieberman and Nestor suggest paying more attention to your breathing, treating it as an essential, yet often unnoticed, aspect of your well-being. The idea is to be aware of your breath, to observe and feel it, almost like a simple form of meditation.

The Problem of Mouth Breathing:
Many people have developed the habit of mouth breathing without realising its negative effects. Mouth breathing can lead to less oxygen intake, which may cause increased fatigue and reduced mental clarity.

Impact on Sleep:
Mouth breathing can negatively affect your sleep quality. It's often linked to problems like snoring, sleep apnea, and general restlessness during the night. Nestor's research suggests that proper nasal breathing can lead to better sleep.

Effect on Immune System:
Breathing through your nose is like a natural filter for your body. It helps keep out harmful pathogens. In contrast, mouth breathing doesn't offer this protection and can be less effective in safeguarding your health.

Improving Nasal Breathing:
You can train yourself to breathe through your nose more often. If you notice yourself mouth breathing, try to consciously switch to nasal breathing. If you have a congested nose, saline sprays can help clear your nasal passages. For those who struggle with mouth breathing at night, nasal strips or other sleep aids can be useful. Engaging in breathing exercises is also a great way to strengthen your nasal breathing habits.

Here are some breathing exercises from practices that have been developed, refined, and passed down through various cultures, traditions, and medical practices over centuries.

1. A simple breathing exercise to help unblock the nose that is based on principles of breath control and physiology that

have been known and used in various forms for many years, particularly within practices like yoga and pranayama.

- Sit in a comfortable position with your back straight.

- Take a small, silent breath in and a small, silent breath out through your nose. It's important these breaths are gentle and through the nose.

- Pinch your nose with your fingers to hold your breath. Nod your head or sway your body gently to keep yourself occupied.

- Hold your breath as long as you can but ensure not to push yourself to the point of discomfort.

- When you need to breathe, release your nose and breathe gently through it, in and out, with control. Avoid deep or forceful breathing after the exercise, as this can bring back the congestion.

- Wait for a minute or so, then repeat this process three to four times until your nose begins to clear.

This technique works by leveraging the body's natural response to increased carbon dioxide levels. This can lead to the dilation of the nasal passages and blood vessels, helping to relieve congestion.

2. Alternate Nostril Breathing (Nadi Shodhana). This technique is aimed at calming the mind, reducing anxiety, and promoting relaxation.

- Sit in a comfortable position. Place the right thumb over the right nostril, inhale deeply through the left nostril. At the peak of inhalation, close off the left nostril with the ring finger, then exhale through the right nostril. Continue the pattern by inhaling through the right nostril and alternating back and forth.

3. Box Breathing (Square Breathing) - Used for concentration and focus, this technique can also help with stress management.

    - Inhale for 4 seconds, hold the breath for 4 seconds, exhale for 4 seconds, and then hold again for 4 seconds. This forms the "box" or "square" pattern of breathing.

4. 4-7-8 Breathing - This is for relaxation and helping to fall asleep. It's said to calm the nervous system.

    - Breathe in quietly through the nose for 4 seconds, hold the breath for 7 seconds, and exhale forcefully through the mouth, pursing the lips and making a "whoosh" sound, for 8 seconds.

5. Nasal Breathing - Emphasises breathing through the nose rather than the mouth to improve oxygenation, humidity, filtration, and temperature control of the inhaled air.

    - Simply ensure that both inhalation and exhalation are done through the nose during daily activities or exercise.

Remember, your breath plays a key role in your health and well-being. Being mindful of your breathing and making small adjustments can have a significant impact on your overall quality of life. With guidance from experts like Lieberman and Nestor, you can explore the full potential of your breath and use it to enhance your daily experiences.

"Expressive writing allows us to step back for a moment and evaluate our lives. Through writing, we can become active creators of our own life stories."
~Dr. James Pennebaker~

Journalling

Consider a healing method, right in front of us, needing only a blank page and a pen. This exceptional remedy doesn't reside in potions or pills but within the practice of journaling. Dr. James Pennebaker, an innovative psychologist, has revealed the incredible healing power of writing on paper. In this exploration of the realm of journaling, we will investigate how this straightforward activity can enhance your mental and physical well-being. We'll explore the science behind it, all while presenting information in a clear and engaging manner, much like a well-maintained journal.

Before we dive into the therapeutic world of journalling, let's get to know the man behind the magic: Dr. James Pennebaker. He's a pioneering psychologist who has spent decades unravelling the mysteries of human expression and its impact on our well-being.

Dr. Pennebaker's journey began in the 1980s when he embarked on a mission to explore the connection between writing and health. Armed with curiosity and a passion for psychology, he conducted groundbreaking studies that revealed the astonishing benefits of expressive writing.

The Pennebaker Paradigm

So, what's the Pennebaker Paradigm all about? It's essentially the belief that by translating our thoughts and emotions into words, we can alleviate stress, boost our mental resilience, and even supercharge our physical health. Think of it as opening a treasure chest of well-being, with a journal as the key.

In one of Dr. Pennebaker's earliest experiments, participants were asked to engage in expressive writing for just 15 minutes a day, four days in a row. The results? Mind-blowing. Those who poured their hearts onto paper reported fewer trips to the doctor, enhanced immune function, and an overall sense of well-being. It's like discovering a fountain of youth, but instead of sipping from it, you're writing your way to a healthier life.

The Healing Power of Words

Why are words so darn powerful? Imagine your mind as a bustling marketplace of thoughts and emotions. Some of them are like unruly vendors, shouting and causing an uproar. When you write, it's like giving these vendors a stage to express themselves.

Writing is your mind's megaphone, allowing these noisy vendors to be heard. Instead of suppressing your thoughts and feelings, you're acknowledging them, making them tangible. It's like bottling up a storm and then finally releasing it. When you externalise your inner world onto paper, you're not just a spectator; you're the conductor of your emotions.

The act of writing grants you a new perspective on your experiences. You're no longer drowning in your feelings; you're surfing on their waves. This shift in viewpoint can be profoundly liberating and therapeutic.

Stress Reduction and Immunity Boost

Stress, the notorious troublemaker, is a part of life. However chronic stress can wear you down mentally and physically. The good news? Journalling can be your stress-busting superhero.

When you write, it can provide a way to release and manage stress. It's not just about expressing your feelings; it's also a means of gaining clarity and finding solutions to life's challenges.

Chronic stress not only affects your mental well-being but can also weaken your immune system. Scientific research has shown that people who maintain a regular writing practice tend to have stronger immune responses. It's like giving your body an added layer of protection against illnesses and infections.

Dealing with Life's Challenges

Life often presents unexpected difficulties and obstacles. That's where journalling comes in as a reliable tool.

Consider life's challenges as unpredictable events. They can be chaotic, disorienting, and overwhelming. Journaling offers a refuge where you can confront and work through these challenges. It's a secure space for expressing your emotions, no matter how turbulent they might be. Through writing, you can navigate these tough situations and ultimately find a sense of calm and resolution.

The Brain-Body Connection

Now, let's explore the fascinating connection between your brain and body when you journal.

Your brain is like the command centre of your body. It sends signals to different systems and organs, and it's exceptionally attuned to your emotional state. When you're stressed or anxious, your brain goes into overdrive, releasing stress hormones like cortisol.

Journalling is like sending your brain a memo, saying, "Hey, we're working on this." As you express your thoughts and emotions, you're telling your brain that you're actively processing your experiences. Your brain, in turn, dials down the stress response.

This communication between your mind and body can lead to lower stress hormone levels, reduced blood pressure, and a more balanced physiological state. It's like flipping a switch from panic mode to relaxation mode.

The Science Behind the Magic

Let's dive deeper into the scientific studies that back up the magic of journalling.

Stress Reduction and Immunity: A study in the Journal of Clinical Psychology found that participants who engaged in expressive writing for four consecutive days experienced reduced stress levels and improved immune function. Writing about their stressors freed up cognitive resources, making it easier for them to cope with stress and maintain a strong immune response.

Emotional Release and Healing: Research from the University of Texas at Austin revealed that expressive writing about traumatic experiences led to increased emotional release. Participants reported greater emotional clarity and closure regarding their traumas, suggesting that writing helps process and resolve deeply rooted emotions.

Improved Mood and Mental Health: Studies at the University of California, Irvine, have shown that individuals who regularly journal report improved mood and reduced symptoms of anxiety and depression. Writing provides a platform for understanding and reframing negative emotions, building emotional resilience over time.

Physical Health Benefits: Researchers at Carnegie Mellon University found that people who wrote about their feelings had a shorter duration of illness when exposed to cold viruses. This indicates that expressive writing can bolster the body's defences against infections.

Enhanced Cognitive Function: Writing helps improve cognitive function and problem-solving skills. By organising thoughts on paper, individuals gain clarity, make better decisions, and become more adept at handling life's challenges.

Making Journalling Work for You

Now that we've explored the science, let's discuss how to make journalling an effective tool in your life.

Choose Your Medium: Whether it's pen and paper or digital journalling, find what suits you best. The key is to make it accessible and comfortable.

Set Aside Time: Dedicate a specific time each day or week for journalling. Consistency is crucial to reaping the full benefits.

Create a Safe Space: Find a quiet, private spot where you can write without distractions. This is your personal haven for self-expression.

Write Freely: When you sit down to write, don't censor yourself. Let your thoughts and emotions flow without judgment. Remember, this is for your eyes only, so be honest and authentic.

Focus on Feelings: While you can write about any topic, it's often most therapeutic to focus on your emotions and experiences. Write about what's bothering you, what's making you happy, or what's on your mind.

Embrace the Process: Understand that journalling is a process, not a quick fix. Over time, you'll notice changes in your mental and physical health, but don't expect immediate results.

Reflect and Learn: Periodically review your journal entries. Notice any patterns, shifts in perspective, or insights you've gained. Journalling can offer valuable self-awareness.

Journalling for Specific Challenges

Journalling can be tailored to address specific challenges or goals in your life. Here are some examples:

Stress Management: If you're feeling overwhelmed, use journalling to identify stressors, explore coping strategies, and track your progress in managing stress.

Grief and Loss: When dealing with the loss of a loved one, write about memories, emotions, and the impact of their absence. Journalling can help you navigate the grieving process.

Anxiety and Depression: For those grappling with anxiety or depression, journalling can help you identify triggers, monitor mood fluctuations, and discover positive activities that boost mental health.

Goal Setting: Use your journal to set and track personal and professional goals. Write about your aspirations, the steps you plan to take, and the progress you make along the way.

Self-Discovery: Journalling is an excellent tool for self-exploration. Write about your values, beliefs, and dreams.

Reflect on your life's journey and the person you want to become.

Journalling as a Lifelong Companion

Journalling is a lifelong companion, ready to walk with you through life's highs and lows. It's a reliable tool for promoting mental and physical health, reducing stress, and helping you navigate challenging times. By giving voice to your thoughts and emotions, you unlock the healing power of words, turning abstract feelings into concrete expressions that can transform your well-being.

Consider your journal as a trusted friend, always there to listen without judgment. It's a place where you can pour out your heart, reflect on your experiences, and gain insight into yourself. Over time, you'll come to appreciate the profound impact of journalling on your overall health and happiness.

As you embark on your journalling journey, remember that there's no right or wrong way to do it. Your journal is a reflection of you, and it can take any form you choose. So, pick up that pen, open a blank document, and start writing. Your words have the power to heal, empower, and transform your life.

In the words of Dr. James Pennebaker, "Write carefully to someone who cares about you. It's amazing how much it can help." So, let your journal be that caring someone, always ready to lend an ear and offer solace, one word at a time.

> *"Mindfulness allows us to see our thoughts and feelings as they really are, freeing us from old ways of thinking."*
>
> *~Daniel J. Siegel~*

Mindfulness: The Art of Being Present

You're sitting in a busy café, sipping your favourite cup of coffee. The aroma wafts through the air, and the chatter of people surrounds you. Your phone pings with messages, your to-do list is a mile long, and your mind is racing with thoughts about work, family, and what's for dinner. In this moment, you're physically present, but your mind is everywhere else. Does this scenario sound familiar?

Now, let's take a journey into the world of mindfulness, an art that can transform moments like these into something truly magical. In the fast pace of daily life, mindfulness is your ticket to experiencing the world with a depth and clarity you never thought possible.

Mindfulness has its roots in ancient Eastern philosophies, particularly Buddhism. It was popularised in the West by Jon Kabat-Zinn, who developed Mindfulness-Based Stress Reduction (MBSR) in the late 1970s.

Jon Kabat-Zinn, the pioneer of MBSR, says, "Mindfulness is awareness that arises through paying attention, on purpose, in the present moment, non-judgmentally."

The Essence of Mindfulness

Mindfulness is about being fully present in the here and now. It's a state of awareness where you engage with each moment without judgment or distraction. Imagine it as a spotlight that shines on the present, revealing its richness and depth.

In a world that never seems to slow down, our thoughts can often wander restlessly, flitting from one idea to another. We find ourselves frequently preoccupied with future plans or past events, seldom fully engaged in the present. Mindfulness serves as a practice that soothes the restless mind, akin to a serene guide gently steering you back to the here and now.

Consider your mind as a vast space. The past and the future are like thoughts waiting to take over. But when you practice mindfulness, you focus solely on the present moment. It's as if you've paused the flow of time, immersing yourself in the intricate details of what's happening right now.

The Beauty of the Present Moment

Now, you might wonder, why is the present moment so special? Well, it's the only moment that truly exists. The past is a memory, and the future is a projection of your imagination. The present is the raw material from which your life is crafted.

When you're mindful, you don't miss out on life's subtle symphony. You hear the rustle of leaves in the wind, feel the warmth of the sun on your skin, and notice the small kindnesses people extend to you. It's like discovering a hidden world within the ordinary, a world that's always been there but often goes unnoticed.

View your life as a sequence of photographs. When you're not fully engaged, the images may appear blurry, lacking in detail and colour. However, through mindfulness, every photo transforms into a vivid masterpiece, preserving the essence of the moment.

The Benefits of Mindfulness

In an environment marked by constant motion and stress, there's a powerful tool for serenity that awaits discovery: mindfulness. It's not merely a trend or a passing social media sensation; it's a transformative practice that can profoundly impact your life. Get ready to explore the incredible benefits of mindfulness on our journey ahead.

1. Blissful Stress Reduction

Consider the following situation: You're caught in an endless traffic jam, your boss has just given you an extremely tight deadline, and your pet has chosen your new shoes as its snack. Stress is creeping in like an unwelcome guest. Yet, there's a solution — mindfulness. It functions as a calming influence for your racing thoughts. By grounding yourself in the present moment, it zaps stress into oblivion.

When you practice mindfulness, you give your mind a vacation from the chaos of the past and the anxiety of the future, landing smack in the lap of the now. Stress, meet your match!

2. Improved Focus and Concentration

Do you ever experience a mind that constantly shifts between thoughts, like a ball bouncing inside a machine? Mindfulness offers you the training to skilfully cultivate your mental presence and awareness. Studies have shown that regular mindfulness practice enhances cognitive functions and memory. It's like upgrading your brain's RAM.

According to Dr. Amishi Jha, a neuroscientist at the University of Miami, "Mindfulness meditation training can help improve working memory, creativity, attention span, and focus." Imagine what you could achieve with a turbocharged brain. That report due tomorrow? Consider it conquered.

3. Emotional Resilience, Thy Name is Mindfulness

Mindfulness is a steadfast partner for emotional resilience. Being mindful helps people develop a better understanding of their emotions and the ability to manage them when faced with the ups and downs of life. By embracing mindfulness, you develop resilience to overcome adversity, nurturing emotional well-being, and resilience in the face of life's challenges.

Tara Brach, a clinical psychologist and mindfulness teacher, says, "Mindfulness allows us to pause and step out of reactive behaviours and old, often painful habit patterns." By stepping back, observing your emotions without judgment, and responding rather than reacting, you become the master of your emotional destiny. That snide comment from a colleague? A mere pebble in the pond of your serenity.

4. Boosted Creativity and Innovation

Ever wondered how those great inventors, artists, and writers conjure up their masterpieces? The answer lies, in part, in mindfulness. When your mind isn't constantly immersed in the tumult of thoughts, creativity flows like a river in full surge.

Sharon Salzberg, a celebrated mindfulness teacher and author, once said, "Mindfulness isn't difficult; we just need to remember to do it." This simple yet profound statement highlights the accessibility of mindfulness. When you practice mindfulness, your mind has the space to venture into new territories of thought. It becomes a dynamic space where innovative ideas can emerge and unexpected connections can be made. In this state of mental clarity and openness, the possibilities for creativity are boundless. It's exciting to think that your next brilliant insight or discovery could emerge from just a moment of mindful breathing. With mindfulness, the journey towards creativity and breakthroughs is not only closer than you think but also enjoyable in its simplicity.

5. Improved Relationships

Remember those times you said something you regretted in the heat of the moment? Mindfulness comes with a magic wand to sprinkle some harmony on your relationships. By being present and truly listening, you can transform your connections.

Psychologist and mindfulness teacher Jack Kornfield emphasises, "When you listen with your whole body and mind, you can deepen your capacity to connect with others." Mindfulness paves the way for empathy, compassion, and understanding. It transforms conversations from arenas of conflict into fields of understanding, where the potential for connection can thrive.

6. Pain Management and Healing

Chronic pain can be an enduring challenge. However, mindfulness provides relief for emotional distress. By directing your attention to the present moment, you can reduce the sensation of discomfort.

The legendary mindfulness researcher and author, Dr. Jon Kabat-Zinn, states, "Mindfulness can be an effective tool in managing chronic pain." Through techniques like body scanning and breath awareness, you can rewire your brain's response to pain, reducing suffering and increasing your quality of life.

7. A Gateway to Gratitude

In the constant pursuit of more, we often forget to savour what we already have. Mindfulness is your ticket to a front-row seat at the theatre of gratitude. It opens your eyes to the beauty of the ordinary.

David Steindl-Rast, a Benedictine monk and interfaith scholar, asserts, "The root of joy is gratefulness." Mindfulness, by its very nature, cultivates gratitude. When you pause to savour your morning coffee, feel the warmth of the sun on your skin, or appreciate the laughter of a loved one, you are practicing mindfulness. And in those moments, you find pure, unadulterated joy.

The Practice of Mindfulness

Now that you're acquainted with the incredible benefits of mindfulness, let's dive into how to make it a part of your daily life.

1. Start Small: Like any skill, mindfulness takes practice. Begin with short sessions, perhaps just a few minutes a day, and gradually increase the duration as you become more comfortable.

2. Find Your Focus: You can practice mindfulness through various methods, including meditation, deep breathing exercises, or simply paying full attention to everyday activities like eating, walking, or even washing the dishes.

Expert Insight: Sharon Salzberg, a renowned mindfulness teacher, advises, "Whatever the present moment contains, accept it as if you had chosen it."

3. Create a Sacred Space: Choose a quiet and comfortable space where you won't be disturbed. It could be a corner of your room or a serene spot in nature.

4. Observe Your Breath: One of the simplest ways to start is by focusing on your breath. Notice the sensation of each inhale and exhale. When your mind wanders, gently bring your focus back to your breath.

5. Be Non-Judgmental: Remember that mindfulness is about observing without judgment. Don't criticise yourself if your mind wanders or if you have intrusive thoughts. It's perfectly normal.

The Mindful Lifestyle

Mindfulness is not just about sitting in meditation; it's about incorporating a mindful approach into every aspect of your life. Here's how you can do that:

1. Mindful Eating: Pay full attention to the flavours, textures, and smells of your food. Chew slowly and savour each bite.

2. Mindful Walking: When you're out for a walk, focus on the sensation of each step, the rustling of leaves, and the feeling of the breeze against your skin.

3. Mindful Listening: When someone is speaking to you, give them your full attention. Put away your phone, make eye contact, and truly listen.

4. Mindful Work: Approach your tasks with mindfulness. Instead of rushing through them, immerse yourself in the process, whether it's typing an email or gardening.

Overcoming Challenges

It's important to acknowledge that mindfulness, like any habit, comes with its challenges. Here's how you can overcome them:

1. Impatience:
You might feel impatient, wanting immediate results. Remember that mindfulness is a journey, and the benefits will accumulate over time.

2. Restless Mind:
It's natural for your mind to wander during mindfulness practice. When it happens, gently bring your focus back to the present moment.

Expert Insight: Zen Master Thich Nhat Hanh suggests, "Feelings come and go like clouds in a windy sky. Conscious breathing is my anchor."

3. The Myth of Time Scarcity:
'Mindfulness demands an exorbitant amount of time'. This misconception often stems from an overly romanticised view of mindfulness as something exclusive to Zen monks or spiritual gurus. The reality is that mindfulness is accessible to all, regardless of how packed our schedules may be.

Mindfulness is not about the quantity of time you invest; it's about the quality of presence you bring to your activities. It's about being fully engaged in the present moment, rather than letting your thoughts scatter in a hundred different directions. Once you understand this, you'll see that even the busiest of schedules can accommodate mindful moments.

4. Mindfulness in Motion: Driving with Awareness

For many of us, commuting is an unavoidable part of daily life. Whether it's a long motorway drive or navigating through city traffic, we often find ourselves stuck behind the wheel. Instead of viewing this time as a wasted opportunity, consider it a prime moment for mindfulness practice.

Focus on Your Breath: Start by bringing your attention to your breath. Feel the rise and fall of your chest as you breathe in and out. Use the rhythm of your breath as an anchor to the present moment. If your mind starts to wander, gently bring it back to your breath.

Observe Sensations: Pay attention to the physical sensations of driving. Feel the steering wheel beneath your hands, the pressure of your foot on the gas pedal or brake, and the vibrations of the engine. Engaging your senses in this way grounds you in the here and now.

Mindful Listening: Use your time in the car to practice mindful listening. Instead of getting lost in radio chatter or your own thoughts, try listening to the sounds around you—the hum of traffic, the rustle of leaves, or the rhythm of rain on the windshield. This practice can be remarkably soothing and can enhance your awareness of the present.

Let Go of Impatience: Traffic jams and unexpected delays can be a breeding ground for frustration. Instead of dwelling on the inconvenience, use these moments to practice patience and acceptance. Embrace the idea that you are exactly where you need to be at this moment.

Gratitude for Movement: When you're stuck in a traffic jam, remind yourself of the privilege of mobility. Many people around the world don't have access to personal transportation. Cultivate gratitude for the ability to travel, even if it means being stuck in traffic occasionally.

5. Mindfulness at Work: Transforming Mundane Tasks

The workplace is another arena where the lack of time is often cited as a barrier to mindfulness. Demanding schedules, deadlines, and the constant barrage of emails can make it challenging to find moments of calm. However, mindfulness can be a powerful tool for improving focus, reducing stress, and increasing productivity at work.

Mindful Breathing: Take short breaks throughout your workday to practice mindful breathing. This can be as simple as taking three deep breaths, focusing your attention on the inhale and exhale. It's a quick reset that can help you regain focus and reduce stress.

Single-Tasking: In a world that glorifies multitasking, mindfulness encourages single-tasking. When you're working on a task, give it your full attention. Avoid the temptation to switch between multiple projects or respond to every notification that pops up on your screen.

Mindful Eating: Use your lunch break as an opportunity to practice mindful eating. Instead of rushing through your meal while checking emails or scrolling through social media, savour each bite. Pay attention to the flavours, textures, and smells of your food.

Mindful Meetings: Meetings can be a source of stress and distraction. Instead of zoning out or worrying about what you'll say next, practice active listening. Focus on what the speaker is saying without judgment or interruption. This not only improves your understanding but also fosters better communication.

Micro-Mindfulness: Integrate micro-mindfulness into your work routine. This involves taking brief moments to check in with yourself. Pause for a minute to notice your body, your breath, and your emotions. It can be particularly beneficial during high-stress moments or when faced with challenging tasks.

The Power of Mindful Technology Use

One of the paradoxes of our digital age is that while technology has the potential to overwhelm us with distractions, it can also be a valuable tool for mindfulness. By using technology mindfully, we can reclaim moments of presence amidst the digital chaos.

Digital Detox: Set aside specific times during the day when you disconnect from digital devices. Use this time to engage in mindful activities such as walking, meditating, or simply enjoying a cup of tea without the distraction of screens.

Mindful App Usage: There are numerous mindfulness apps available that can guide you through short meditation sessions or provide mindfulness reminders throughout the day. These apps can help you build a consistent mindfulness practice, even in the busiest of schedules.

Screen Breaks: Incorporate screen breaks into your work routine. Every hour, take a few minutes to step away from your computer or phone. Close your eyes, stretch, and take a few mindful breaths to reset your focus and reduce eye strain.

Mindful Social Media: When scrolling through social media, practice mindfulness by consciously observing your reactions to posts. Are they generating positive or negative emotions? Are you mindlessly comparing yourself to others? Being aware of these patterns can help you use social media more intentionally.

The Ripple Effect

When you embrace mindfulness, you're not just transforming your own life; you're creating a ripple effect of positivity that can touch the lives of those around you. Your newfound sense of calm and presence can inspire others to do the same.

Expert Insight: Jack Kornfield, a mindfulness teacher, emphasises, "If your compassion does not include yourself, it is incomplete."

Mindfulness is a simple yet profound practice that has the power to enhance every aspect of your life. By being present in the moment, you can reduce stress, improve your emotional well-being, and even boost your physical health.

Remember to start small, find your focus, and be patient with yourself. The journey of mindfulness is a lifelong one, and every moment you spend in awareness brings you closer to a more fulfilling and peaceful life.

So, why wait? Start your mindfulness journey today. Take a few moments to sit quietly, breathe deeply, and become fully present in this moment. You'll be amazed at the transformation it brings to your life.

> *"The connection between the gut and brain is significant; what we eat can uplift or depress us."*
>
> ~Dr. John J. Ratey~

From Plate to Peace

The Interplay of Nutrition and Mental Wellness

The old saying, "You are what you eat," holds more truth than we often realise, especially when it comes to our mental well-being. In an era where the pace of life is frenetic, and stress and anxiety seem to lurk around every corner, the significance of foods, supplements, and vitamins in maintaining our mental health has never been more apparent.

The correlation between food and mental state is profound. Junk food, typically high in ultra processed ingredients, saturated fat, and sugar, has been linked to a range of detrimental effects on the brain and behaviour.

Notably, it can impair cognitive function, encompassing memory, attention, and decision-making, largely attributed to factors such as inflammation, oxidative stress, and alterations in brain structure. Furthermore, the consumption of junk food has been associated with an elevated risk of developing mental health disorders like depression and anxiety, driven by complex mechanisms including inflammation, changes in brain chemistry, and compromised gut health.

Beyond these long-term consequences, immediate effects include reduced mood and energy levels, heightened irritability and aggression, as well as poor sleep quality, all stemming from factors like fluctuating blood sugar levels, inflammation, and the release of stress hormones. In essence, the quality of our diet has a profound impact on our mental well-being, emphasising the importance of mindful food choices for a healthier mind.

Curious fact about junk food: In 2018, a man in the United Kingdom was acquitted of a robbery charge after his defence team argued that his consumption of junk food had impaired his judgment and self-control.

Our brains, those intricate command centres that orchestrate our thoughts, emotions, and behaviours, are remarkably sensitive to the nutrients we consume. Every bite we take and every sip we swallow can influence our mood, cognitive function, and overall mental well-being. This section delves into the relationship between nutrition and mental health, highlighting how what we eat significantly affects our psychological well-being.

From the sunshine vitamin, vitamin D, to the brain-boosting omega-3 fatty acids found in fatty fish, we'll explore the vital role of specific vitamins and nutrients in regulating mood and cognitive function. We'll explore the science behind these nutritional powerhouses, uncovering the remarkable studies that link them to improved mental health.

Moreover, we'll shine a light on the hidden heroes of our plates— the antioxidants, the probiotics, and the spices that not only nourish our bodies but also protect our brains from the ravages of stress and inflammation. We'll reveal how the gut-brain connection, a growing field of research, emphasises the importance of a healthy digestive system in maintaining mental equilibrium.

During our journey, we'll learn that food is more than just something we eat; it's like medicine for our thoughts and feelings. Also, if we use supplements and vitamins the right way and with expert advice, they can help make our minds stronger.

Get ready for a deep dive into the world of foods, supplements, and vitamins that promote mental well-being. Together, we'll uncover methods to care for both our body and mind, leading to a brighter, stronger, and more balanced life.

Vitamin D: The Sunshine Vitamin

When it comes to mental health, vitamin D is a superstar. This essential vitamin, often referred to as the "sunshine vitamin," plays a crucial role in maintaining not only our physical health but also our mental wellbeing.

Vitamin D is a fat-soluble vitamin that plays a vital role in numerous bodily functions. While it's well-known for its importance in maintaining healthy bones by aiding calcium absorption, its significance extends into diverse realms of human health, particularly mental wellbeing.

Vitamin D is produced in our skin when exposed to sunlight, and it's involved in various processes in the body, including the production of serotonin, a neurotransmitter that regulates mood. Studies have shown that low levels of vitamin D are associated with an increased risk of depression and other mood disorders. One study published in the Journal of Clinical Psychiatry found that individuals with low levels of vitamin D were more likely to experience symptoms of depression.

Furthermore, vitamin D has been linked to cognitive function. A study published in JAMA Neurology revealed that older adults with low vitamin D levels had a higher risk of cognitive decline. This suggests that maintaining optimal vitamin D levels through sunlight exposure or supplements may not only boost your mood but also help preserve your cognitive abilities.

So, how can you get your daily dose of vitamin D? Aside from soaking up the sun, you can find it in foods like fatty fish (salmon, mackerel, and trout), fortified dairy products, and supplements. It's essential to consult with a healthcare professional to determine the right dosage for your individual needs.

Omega-3 Fatty Acids: Brain Boosters

Omega-3 fatty acids are a group of polyunsaturated fats that have gained significant attention for their potential benefits for mental health. The two main types of omega-3s found in food are eicosapentaenoic acid (EPA) and docosahexaenoic acid (DHA).

These fatty acids play a crucial role in brain development and function. In fact, DHA is a major component of the brain's cell membranes. Research suggests that omega-3 fatty acids may have a positive impact on conditions such as depression, anxiety, and attention deficit hyperactivity disorder (ADHD).

A study published in the Journal of Clinical Psychiatry found that individuals with higher levels of omega-3 fatty acids in their blood were less likely to experience symptoms of depression. Another study published in the Journal of the American Medical Association (JAMA) Pediatrics showed that children with higher DHA levels in their blood had a lower risk of developing ADHD.

The best dietary sources of omega-3 fatty acids are fatty fish like salmon, sardines, and trout. If you're not a fan of seafood, you can also obtain these essential fatty acids from flaxseeds, chia seeds, and walnuts. Additionally, omega-3 supplements are available, typically in the form of fish oil capsules or algae-based options for vegetarians and vegans.

Nuts and seeds are packed with nutrients that can benefit your mental health. They are excellent sources of healthy fats, including omega-3 fatty acids. These healthy fats are essential for brain health and mood regulation.

Additionally, nuts and seeds are rich in minerals like magnesium and zinc, both of which play roles in mental well-being. Zinc, in particular, is involved in neurotransmitter regulation and has been linked to reduced symptoms of depression.

A handful of almonds, walnuts, or pumpkin seeds can make for a satisfying and brain-boosting snack. You can also incorporate them into your meals or sprinkle them on salads and yogurt.

Curious Fact: Did you know that the Inuit people of Greenland, who consume a diet rich in Omega-3s from fatty fish, have remarkably low rates of depression and mood disorders?

Magnesium: The Relaxation Mineral

Magnesium is a mineral that plays a crucial role in over 300 biochemical reactions in the body, including those related to brain function and mental health. It's often referred to as the "relaxation mineral" because of its role in relaxing muscles and calming the nervous system.

Low levels of magnesium have been associated with increased stress and anxiety. A study published in PLOS ONE found that magnesium supplementation improved symptoms of depression and anxiety in adults with low magnesium levels. Another study published in the "Journal of Research in Medical Sciences" found that magnesium supplementation can significantly reduce symptoms of anxiety and depression. This mineral plays a vital role in regulating stress hormones like cortisol.

Magnesium-rich foods include nuts, seeds, leafy greens, and whole grains. Incorporating these foods into your diet can help ensure you're getting enough magnesium to support your mental well-being.

Curious Fact: Ancient Greeks bathed in "Epsom salts" rich in magnesium to relax and rejuvenate their minds and bodies. Today, you can still enjoy the benefits by taking Epsom salt baths.

B Vitamins: The Mood Regulators

The B-vitamins, a group of water-soluble vitamins, are essential for overall health, including mental wellbeing. They play a crucial role in various brain functions, including the synthesis of neurotransmitters that regulate mood.

Vitamin B12, in particular, is often associated with mental health. A deficiency in this vitamin can lead to symptoms such as fatigue, irritability, and even depression. A study published in the Journal of Psychiatric Research found that individuals with lower levels of vitamin B12 were more likely to experience depressive symptoms.

Folate, another B-vitamin, is also important for mental health. It's involved in the production of serotonin, a neurotransmitter that regulates mood. Research published in the American Journal of Clinical Nutrition suggests that individuals with higher folate intake have a lower risk of developing depression.

Dark leafy greens like spinach, kale, and Swiss chard are nutritional powerhouses when it comes to mental health. They are rich in folate, a B-vitamin that plays a crucial role in the production of neurotransmitters like serotonin.

In addition to folate, dark leafy greens contain other essential nutrients like iron and magnesium, which are important for overall brain health. Iron helps transport oxygen to the brain, ensuring it functions optimally, while magnesium, as mentioned earlier, has a calming effect on the nervous system.

Including a variety of dark leafy greens in your diet not only supports your mental health but also provides a wide range of vitamins and minerals essential for your well-being.

Science and Eye-Opening Discoveries

Folate and Depression: A Brighter Outlook: In a meta-analysis published in "JAMA Psychiatry" (Gilbody et al., 2007), folate supplementation emerged as a promising strategy to reduce depressive symptoms, especially in individuals with low folate levels.

Vitamin B12 and Schizophrenia: Research in the "American Journal of Psychiatry" (Gracious et al., 2012) suggests that vitamin B12 supplementation might help manage symptoms in some individuals with schizophrenia, offering a glimmer of hope for those facing severe mental health challenges.

Vitamin B6: Soothing Anxiety: A study in "The Journal of Clinical Psychiatry" (Roohani et al., 2018) uncovered a link between vitamin B6 intake and reduced anxiety scores. It's like having a secret weapon against life's worries.

To ensure you're getting enough B-vitamins for optimal mental health, incorporate foods like lean meats, poultry, fish, eggs, dairy products, leafy greens, and whole grains into your diet. If you have concerns about your B-vitamin intake, consult with a healthcare professional to discuss supplementation.

Antioxidants: Brain-Protecting Superheroes

Antioxidants are compounds that help protect our brain cells from oxidative stress and inflammation, both of which are linked to mental health disorders like depression and anxiety.

One group of antioxidants that has received a lot of attention is flavonoids. These plant compounds are found in various fruits and vegetables and have been shown to have neuroprotective properties. A study published in The American Journal of Clinical Nutrition found that higher flavonoid intake was associated with a reduced risk of depression.

Foods rich in antioxidants, such as berries, dark chocolate, and green tea, can be a tasty way to support your mental health. Incorporating a variety of colourful fruits and vegetables into your diet can provide a diverse range of antioxidants that your brain will thank you for.

Blueberries, the pint-sized dynamos, are hailed as "brain berries" for their outstanding cognitive perks. These tiny marvels are bursting with antioxidants and phytochemicals that protect and enhance your brain's performance.

Curious Fact: The deep blue hue of blueberries is a telltale sign of their powerful antioxidants, particularly anthocyanins. These compounds enhance memory, improve cognitive function, and even stave off age-related cognitive decline.

Blueberries can be your brain's best friend, whether enjoyed as a snack, blended into smoothies, or sprinkled atop oatmeal and yogurt. Their delightful taste is just the cherry on top of their mental health benefits.

Dark Chocolate is not just a treat for your palate but also a boon for your brain and mood.

Curious Fact: Dark chocolate contains a compound called theobromine, which can have a stimulating effect on your mood and energy levels, much like caffeine but without the jitters.

Scientific Evidence: A study published in "The Journal of Psychopharmacology" reported that consuming dark chocolate with a high cocoa content significantly improved mood, reducing feelings of stress in participants. It's a sweet indulgence with genuine benefits!

Green Tea: L-Theanine Magic

Green tea contains an amino acid called L-theanine, a tranquiliser for your brain. It possesses the remarkable ability to promote relaxation and sharpen focus without inducing drowsiness.

Curious Fact: L-theanine is the wizard behind green tea's soothing and focusing effects. It doesn't just calm the storm; it helps you navigate it with clarity. Researchers have even found that L-theanine supplements enhance attention and cognitive performance.

Green tea is a treasure chest not only for L-theanine but also for catechins, antioxidants that shield your brain from aging and cognitive disorders. Sip on green tea throughout the day to infuse your life with mental acuity.

Probiotics: Gut-Brain Connection

Did you know that there is a strong connection between your gut and your brain? The gut-brain axis is a bidirectional communication system between the gastrointestinal tract and the central nervous system. This connection has a significant impact on mental health.

Probiotics are beneficial bacteria that help maintain a healthy gut microbiome. Research has shown that a balanced gut microbiome is associated with improved mood and reduced symptoms of depression and anxiety. A study published in the journal General Psychiatry found that individuals who consumed probiotics experienced fewer symptoms of depression and anxiety compared to those who did not. A groundbreaking study published in "Psychopharmacology" demonstrated that participants who consumed probiotics experienced reduced anxiety and altered brain activity in regions associated with emotion and sensation.

You can find probiotics in fermented foods like yogurt, kefir, kimchi, and sauerkraut. Additionally, probiotic supplements are available for those looking to boost their gut health.

Curious Fact: The gut is often referred to as the "second brain" because it communicates directly with the central nervous system and influences your mood, stress response, and even decision-making.

Whole Grains: Complex Carbohydrates for Steady Energy

Carbohydrates are often demonised in popular diets, but they are essential for maintaining stable energy levels and supporting mental health. Whole grains, in particular, provide a steady source of energy and can help regulate mood.

Whole grains like oats, quinoa, brown rice, and whole wheat bread are rich in fibre, which slows down the absorption of carbohydrates and helps prevent blood sugar spikes and crashes. Stable blood sugar levels are crucial for maintaining mood stability and preventing irritability and mood swings.

Incorporating a variety of whole grains into your diet can help you maintain steady energy levels throughout the day, keeping your mind sharp and your mood stable.

Turmeric and Curcumin: The Golden Spices

Spices can do more than just add flavour to your dishes; they can also have a positive impact on your mental health. Turmeric, in particular, contains a compound called curcumin, which has potent anti-inflammatory and antioxidant properties.

Research suggests that curcumin may be effective in managing symptoms of depression and anxiety. A study published in the Journal of Affective Disorders found that individuals who took curcumin supplements experienced significant improvements in mood compared to a placebo group.

Turmeric is a versatile spice that can be used in a variety of dishes, from curries to smoothies. Including it in your diet may provide both flavour and mental health benefits.

Lean Protein: Amino Acids for Neurotransmitters

Protein is composed of amino acids, the building blocks of neurotransmitters that influence mood and mental health. Consuming an adequate amount of lean protein can help ensure your body has the amino acids it needs to produce these essential brain chemicals.

Curious Fact: Tryptophan, an amino acid found in protein-rich foods like poultry, turkey, and tofu, is a precursor to serotonin, the "feel-good" neurotransmitter. Ensuring a steady intake of tryptophan through your diet can help support a stable mood.

Additionally, lean protein sources are also rich in other essential nutrients like vitamin B12, which we discussed earlier, and iron, which is crucial for oxygen transport to the brain.

Water: Hydration for Cognitive Function

Last but certainly not least, we must not overlook the importance of hydration for mental health. Water is essential for the proper functioning of the brain, and even mild dehydration can impair cognitive function, concentration, and mood.

Studies have shown that dehydration can lead to increased feelings of tension and anxiety. To maintain optimal mental health, it's essential to stay adequately hydrated throughout the day.

While we often focus on food and supplements, ensuring you drink enough water is a simple yet crucial step in supporting your mental well-being.

In the fascinating world of supplements, vitamins, and foods for mental health, we've explored an array of nutrients and their impact on our well-being. From the sunshine vitamin, vitamin D, to the brain-boosting omega-3 fatty acids, and the mood-regulating B-vitamins, these nutritional elements are essential for maintaining a healthy mind.

While these dietary components are indeed powerful tools for enhancing mental health, it's important to remember that they work best as part of a balanced diet and lifestyle. Combining these nutritional elements with regular exercise, stress management techniques, and a good night's sleep can have a profound impact on your overall mental well-being.

Remember before you take any supplements or vitamins consult with a healthcare professional or registered dietitian to ensure it is the right move for you. By nourishing your body with the right nutrients, you can embark on a journey towards a happier, more resilient, and mentally vibrant life. So, start exploring the colourful world of foods that can nourish your mind and uplift your spirits today. Your brain will thank you for it!

Self-Test: Nutrition and Mental Health Assessment

This self-test is designed to help you evaluate how your current dietary habits may be influencing your mental health. Answer each question honestly for the most accurate assessment.

Instructions:
For each statement, select the option that best describes your typical dietary habits and mental health experiences. Use the following scale:

Often:
This applies to me most of the time or daily.

Sometimes:
This applies to me occasionally or a few times a week.

Rarely:
This applies to me seldom or almost never.

Questions	O	S	R
I eat a variety of foods including fruits, vegetables, whole grains, lean proteins, and healthy fats.			
I consume omega-3 rich foods (such as fatty fish, flaxseeds, walnuts) or supplements.			
I drink enough water throughout the day to stay properly hydrated.			
I consume processed or high-sugar foods (such as fast food, soda, sweets).			
I get sufficient sunlight exposure or consume foods/supplements rich in Vitamin D.			
I include foods high in B-vitamins (such as leafy greens, legumes, and whole grains) in my meals.			
I consume magnesium-rich foods (such as nuts, seeds, and leafy greens).			
I eat regular meals and snacks to maintain stable energy levels throughout the day.			
I experience mood swings or irritability that I can't attribute to other causes.			
I maintain a good level of concentration and mental focus throughout the day.			

Scoring:

Add up the number of times you selected each response.
Interpretation:

Predominantly 'Often':
You are likely nourishing your body in a way that supports mental health. Continue your balanced dietary habits to maintain your mental well-being.

Predominantly 'Sometimes':
Your diet may sometimes support your mental health, but there's room for improvement. Focus on increasing the frequency of healthy eating habits.

Predominantly 'Rarely':
Your current diet may not be adequately supporting your mental health. Consider incorporating more nutrient-rich foods and consistent meal patterns.

> *"Self-care is so much more than a beauty regimen or an external thing you do. It has to start within your heart to know what you need to navigate your life. A pedicure doesn't last, but meditating every day does.*
>
> ~Carrie Anne Moss~

Embracing Self-Care

In this world where we're constantly juggling multiple responsibilities, the concept of self-care has gained significant attention, and for good reason. It serves as the foundation upon which a life of well-being, balance, and fulfilment is built. Self-care is not just a passing trend; it is a deeply rooted practice that transcends cultures, generations, and individual circumstances. Here we are discussing the very essence of self-care, uncovering what it truly means and why it is of paramount importance in our lives.

At its core, self-care is a conscious and deliberate act of taking care of yourself across physical, emotional, and mental dimensions. It is a proactive approach to nurturing and preserving your overall health and well-being. While self-care encompasses a vast array of activities and practices, ranging from simple daily rituals to more structured routines, its essence remains constant: prioritising yourself so that you can thrive in every aspect of your life.

Scientific Insight: A study published in the "Journal of Health Psychology" (Boswell, A. A., et al., 2018) demonstrated a strong correlation between regular self-care practices and improved psychological well-being. Participants who engaged in self-care reported reduced stress levels and enhanced overall life satisfaction.

Physical Self-Care

The physical dimension of self-care is the bedrock upon which our overall well-being stands. It encompasses a wide range of activities and practices dedicated to nurturing and sustaining our physical health, ensuring that our bodies remain strong, resilient, and ready to face life's challenges. Now, we will delve deeper into the significance of physical self-care, exploring not only its importance but also the science behind its profound impact on our lives.

Scientific Insight: A landmark study conducted by researchers at Harvard Medical School (Holt-Lunstad, J., et al., 2010) found compelling evidence supporting the vital role of social connections in physical self-care. The study revealed that individuals with strong social relationships had a significantly lower risk of mortality compared to those with weaker or fewer social ties. This remarkable connection between social connections and physical well-being underscores the holistic nature of self-care.

The physical dimension of self-care encompasses various practices, and at its core, it is about cultivating habits that prioritise your body's health and vitality:

Regular Exercise: Engaging in physical activity is one of the cornerstones of physical self-care. Exercise not only strengthens your muscles and cardiovascular system but also releases endorphins—natural mood lifters. Whether it's a brisk walk, a yoga session, or an intense workout at the gym, finding an exercise routine that suits your preferences is crucial for maintaining physical well-being.

Balanced Nutrition: Proper nutrition is another vital aspect of physical self-care. Consuming a well-balanced diet rich in nutrients provides your body with the fuel it needs to function optimally. It not only supports physical health but also has a profound impact on mental and emotional well-being, as discussed before.

Adequate Hydration: Staying hydrated is often overlooked but is essential for overall health. Water plays a fundamental role in nearly every bodily function, from regulating body temperature to aiding digestion and circulation. Ensuring you drink enough water throughout the day is a simple yet powerful form of physical self-care.

Quality Sleep: The importance of sleep cannot be overstated. Quality restorative sleep is a cornerstone of physical and mental health. It is during sleep that your body repairs and rejuvenates itself, contributing to overall well-being. Creating a sleep-friendly environment and adhering to a regular sleep schedule are essential components of physical self-care.

Regular Health Check-Ups: Monitoring your physical health through regular check-ups with healthcare professionals is a proactive form of self-care. It allows for early detection and prevention of potential health issues, ensuring that you receive timely treatment and support.

The significance of physical self-care extends beyond the physical realm. It has a profound impact on our emotional and mental well-being as well. Engaging in regular physical activity, for example, has been shown to reduce symptoms of anxiety and depression, boost self-esteem, and improve overall mood. Additionally, a balanced diet rich in essential nutrients can enhance cognitive function, contributing to mental clarity and emotional stability.

Physical self-care is not a one-size-fits-all approach. It involves tuning into your body's unique needs and preferences. Listening to your body's signals, such as hunger, thirst, and fatigue, and responding with care and attention is a fundamental aspect of this dimension of self-care. It's about building a positive and supportive relationship with your body, one that fosters well-being and longevity.

Emotional Self-Care

The emotional dimension of self-care is a profound exploration into the realm of our feelings, emotions, and the intricate web of our inner world. It encompasses practices and strategies that enable us to understand, manage, and nurture our emotional well-being. In this section, we'll investigate deep into the emotional aspect of self-care, exploring not only its significance but also the scientific insights that shed light on its transformative power.

Scientific Insight: A notable study published in the "Journal of Positive Psychology" (Wood, A. M., et al., 2010) highlighted the positive correlation between acts of kindness directed towards oneself and emotional well-being. This research emphasised that practices like self-compassion and self-forgiveness have a profound impact on our emotional state, leading to increased life satisfaction and overall happiness.

The emotional dimension of self-care is rooted in recognising, acknowledging, and honouring your emotions. It's about fostering emotional resilience, understanding your feelings, and navigating the ups and downs of life in a healthy and constructive way. Here are some key components of emotional self-care:

Emotional Awareness: The first step in emotional self-care is becoming attuned to your emotions. This involves recognising and acknowledging your feelings without judgment. It's about creating a safe and accepting space within yourself to experience and express your emotions authentically.

Emotional Expression: Emotions are meant to be felt and expressed. Bottling up feelings can lead to emotional distress. Engaging in healthy outlets for emotional expression, such as journalling, talking to a trusted friend or therapist, or engaging in creative pursuits, can be incredibly therapeutic.

Stress Management: Stress is a natural part of life, but chronic stress can take a toll on your emotional well-being. Practicing stress management techniques, such as mindfulness meditation, deep breathing exercises, or yoga, can help you cope with stress more effectively and maintain emotional equilibrium.

Self-Compassion: Treating yourself with the same kindness and understanding that you offer to others is a fundamental aspect of emotional self-care. Self-compassion involves recognising your own worth and extending love and support to yourself during challenging times.

Emotional Boundaries: Establishing healthy emotional boundaries is essential for emotional self-care. It involves recognising your limits, learning to say no when necessary, and communicating your emotional needs with clarity.

The impact of emotional self-care extends beyond individual well-being; it also influences your relationships with others. When you practice emotional self-care, you're better equipped to communicate effectively, empathise with others, and maintain healthier relationships. Emotionally resilient individuals are more adept at handling conflicts, expressing their needs, and offering support to loved ones.

Emotional self-care also plays a pivotal role in mental health. Research has shown that individuals who practice self-compassion and self-forgiveness are less prone to depression, anxiety, and other mental health challenges. By nurturing your emotional well-being, you build a strong foundation for your mental health.

In essence, emotional self-care is a profound journey into the heart of your emotions. It's about developing a compassionate and supportive relationship with yourself, one that empowers you to navigate life's emotional complexities with grace and resilience. It's a reminder that your feelings are valid, and caring for your emotional well-being is an act of self-love and self-respect.

As we continue our exploration of self-care, we'll delve into the mental dimension. The emotional, mental, and physical dimensions of self-care are interconnected, forming a holistic approach to nurturing your well-being. Remember, your emotional health is a precious asset, and by embracing the emotional dimension of self-care, you embark on a journey toward greater emotional resilience, authenticity, and inner peace.

Mental Self-Care

The mental dimension of self-care delves into the intricacies of our cognitive and intellectual well-being. It's about nurturing your mind, maintaining mental clarity, managing stress, and fostering your intellectual growth. Here, we will explore the profound importance of mental self-care and the scientific insights that illuminate its transformative power.

Scientific Insight: Research conducted at the University of California, Berkeley (Fredrickson, B. L., et al., 2008) has shed light on the connection between cultivating positive emotions and mental self-care. The study revealed that engaging in activities that generate positive emotions, such as mindfulness meditation, not only enhances cognitive functioning but also leads to improvements in overall mental well-being.

The mental dimension of self-care encompasses a wide array of practices aimed at nurturing your cognitive and emotional intelligence. Here are key aspects of mental self-care:
Mindfulness and Meditation: Mindfulness meditation is a powerful mental self-care practice. It involves paying focused, non-judgmental attention to the present moment. This practice

can help reduce stress, improve concentration, and promote emotional balance. As we discussed earlier.

Stress Management: Stress can take a toll on your mental well-being. Engaging in stress management techniques such as relaxation exercises, time management, and prioritisation can help you navigate life's challenges with a clear mind.

Learning and Intellectual Stimulation: Continuous learning and intellectual engagement are essential for mental self-care. Reading, pursuing hobbies, taking up new challenges, and seeking out new experiences can stimulate your mind and boost cognitive function.

Emotional Regulation: The ability to recognise and manage your emotions is crucial for mental self-care. Practices such as emotional regulation techniques and self-reflection can help you navigate emotional challenges with resilience.

Positive Self-Talk: Cultivating a positive inner dialogue is fundamental for mental self-care. Self-compassion, self-affirmation, and self-empowerment are practices that promote a healthy self-image and emotional well-being.

Creative Expression: Engaging in creative pursuits, whether it's writing, art, music, or any other form of self-expression, is a means of channelling your thoughts and emotions constructively. It fosters creativity and emotional release.

The mental dimension of self-care is intimately connected to your emotional well-being. By cultivating positive emotions and emotional intelligence, you not only enhance your mental clarity but also improve your overall emotional resilience. This holistic approach to self-care recognises that the mind and emotions are interconnected, and nurturing one aspect positively affects the other.

Moreover, mental self-care plays a pivotal role in enhancing your cognitive functioning. A clear and focused mind is better equipped to problem-solve, make decisions, and adapt to life's challenges. It can lead to increased creativity, improved memory, and enhanced decision-making abilities.

Scientific Insight: Studies conducted by the American Psychological Association (APA) emphasise the profound impact of self-care on mental health. Individuals who actively engage in mental self-care practices are better equipped to cope with stress, reduce the risk of mental health issues, and experience greater overall well-being.

In essence, the mental dimension of self-care is about nurturing your mind, managing your thoughts and emotions, and fostering your intellectual growth. It's a practice that promotes mental clarity, emotional resilience, and cognitive vitality. By embracing mental self-care, you empower yourself to navigate life's complexities with grace, creativity, and a clear sense of purpose.

Creating Your Personalised Self-Care Plan

Here, we embark on a crucial step in your self-care journey: creating a personalised self-care plan. By now, you've gained insights into the physical, emotional, and mental dimensions of self-care, learned practical strategies, and tackled common challenges. Now it's time to weave all these elements together into a cohesive and tailored self-care plan that aligns with your unique needs and goals.

Step 1: Self-Assessment

Begin by reflecting on your current self-care practices and well-being. Consider the following questions:

What areas of self-care are you already addressing well?
In which dimensions—physical, emotional, or mental—do you feel the most imbalance or challenges?
What self-care practices resonate most with you?
What self-care practices have you found challenging to maintain consistently?
This self-assessment helps you gain clarity about your starting point and areas that need more attention.

Step 2: Define Your Goals

Identify specific goals you want to achieve through your self-care plan. Your goals should be specific. For example, rather than setting a vague goal like "improve my mental health," you might set a SMART goal like "practice mindfulness meditation for 10 minutes every morning for the next month to reduce stress and enhance focus."

Step 3: Prioritise Self-Care Dimensions

Considering your self-assessment and goals, prioritise the dimensions of self-care that require the most attention. For instance, if you're experiencing high levels of stress, emotional self-care might be your top priority. Alternatively, if you're aiming to enhance cognitive function, mental self-care may take precedence.

Step 4: Choose Self-Care Practices

Now, select specific self-care practices that align with your goals and chosen dimensions. Ensure that these practices resonate with you personally. Your self-care plan should be enjoyable and sustainable. For example:

If physical self-care is a priority, choose exercise routines you enjoy, whether it's dancing, hiking, or yoga.
For emotional self-care, consider journaling, talking to a therapist, or practicing self-compassion.
In the realm of mental self-care, explore mindfulness meditation, reading, or creative activities.

Step 5: Create a Schedule

Integrate your chosen self-care practices into your daily or weekly schedule. Allocate dedicated time for each practice. Treat these appointments with the same importance as other commitments. Scheduling helps ensure that self-care becomes a consistent part of your routine.

Step 6: Stay Flexible and Adaptable

Life is dynamic, and circumstances change. Be prepared to adapt your self-care plan as needed. If a particular practice no longer serves you or your goals shift, don't hesitate to make adjustments. Flexibility is key to sustaining self-care in the long term.

Step 7: Monitor and Evaluate

Regularly assess your progress and the impact of your self-care practices on your well-being. Are you moving closer to your goals? Are there practices that need refinement or replacement? Self-reflection helps you fine-tune your self-care plan for maximum effectiveness.

Step 8: Seek Support and Accountability

Consider sharing your self-care plan with a trusted friend, family member, or therapist. They can provide support and hold you accountable. Joining a self-care group or community can also offer valuable encouragement and motivation.

Step 9: Celebrate Success

Acknowledge and celebrate your self-care achievements, no matter how small. Self-care is a journey, and every step forward is a victory. Celebrating your successes reinforces your commitment to well-being.

Step 10: Be Kind to Yourself

Finally, remember that self-care is an act of self-love and self-compassion. Treat yourself with kindness, patience, and understanding. If you stumble or face setbacks, it's okay. Self-care is about resilience, growth, and nurturing your holistic well-being over time.

By following these steps and creating your personalised self-care plan, you embark on a journey toward a more balanced, fulfilling, and resilient life. Your self-care plan is a living document that can evolve as you grow and your needs change. Embrace the power of self-care as a lifelong practice that empowers you to thrive in every dimension of your well-being.

Self-care is not a luxury; it's a necessity for a healthy and fulfilling life. This book has explored the science behind self-care, delving into its physical, emotional, and mental dimensions. By integrating evidence-based practices into your daily routine, you can experience the transformative power of self-care. Remember, your well-being matters, and you have the tools to nurture it. Start your journey towards a healthier, happier you today.

> *"Nothing lights up the brain like play."*
> *~Dr. Stuart Brown~*

The Power of Play

Rediscovering the world with the fresh, enthusiastic perspective of a child can be exhilarating. Think about the excitement in a game of tag or the creativity involved in crafting imaginary worlds. This excitement stems from the power of play, a vital yet often overlooked aspect of life. Play is not just an activity for children; it's a fundamental part of human development at all ages. It's not just for fun; it's how we first learn to understand the world and our place in it. Play is a key to happiness, contributing to joy and well-being throughout life. It's an essential element that adds excitement and meaning to our existence.

Magnuson and Barnett, in their groundbreaking 2013 study, presented the concept of 'the playful advantage.' They didn't just suggest but empirically demonstrated how engaging in playful activities creates a ripple effect in an adult's physiological and psychological well-being. Play, with its inherent ability to stimulate a sense of casual ease and enjoyment, acts as a counterbalance to the rigidity that daily stressors impose on our minds and bodies. It encourages a mental state where laughter comes easily, creativity flourishes, and problems are nothing more than the next playful challenge to overcome.

Rene Proyer's work in 2013 provided a fresh perspective, linking playfulness with the often-elusive concept of personal well-being and happiness in adults. Proyer's research highlighted that playful adults have a particular flair for transforming mundane tasks into enjoyable experiences, seeing life through a lens of curiosity and wonder that most people lose in their transition to adulthood. This attitude doesn't just colour their world more vibrantly; it significantly enhances their personal relationships, job satisfaction, and overall contentment with life.

But how does one reclaim this sense of playfulness? It starts with allowing oneself to experience the present fully, finding humour in everyday situations, and not shying away from the occasional silliness. It's about breaking away from the fetters of 'always acting your age' and permitting yourself moments of unadulterated joy, just for the sake of it.

The term 'playful adult' often conjures images of irresponsibility or immaturity. This misconception, however, couldn't be further from the truth—a fact that Guitard, Ferland, and Dutil illuminated in their 2005 study. They painted a picture of adult playfulness as a trait brimming with positivity, one that embraces a light-hearted approach to life, balancing the seriousness imposed by adult responsibilities.

Being playful isn't about neglecting responsibilities, but about approaching them with a creative, vibrant spirit. It's the ability to turn challenges into opportunities for engagement, finding joy in tasks that others might find tedious. This mindset doesn't just elevate personal happiness; it also enhances problem-solving skills and promotes a supportive environment at home and work.

Adults, entangled in responsibilities, often sideline their creative passions, regarding them as mere hobbies. Zhang and Li's 2014 review turned this notion on its head, establishing play as a critical catalyst for creativity and exploration in adulthood. Engaging in playful activities isn't a diversion from serious learning but rather a path to it.

When adults allow themselves to play—be it dabbling in arts, playing musical instruments, or even immersing in video games—they ignite the parts of their brain responsible for creativity and learning. This engagement leads to more innovative thinking, better adaptability to change, and even enhanced memory. Essentially, when adults play, they're not retreating into a child's world; they're nurturing their intellect and emotional health.

Dr. Stuart Brown, a renowned researcher in the field of play, took the understanding of adult play to new horizons. His extensive studies and observations concluded that play is not just beneficial but essential for adults, impacting everything from personal health to social interactions.

According to Dr. Brown, play is the very mechanism that allows adults to keep their curiosity alive, tackle challenges with optimism, and remain resilient in the face of adversity. He emphasised that the opposite of play isn't work—it's depression. Without play, adults risk more than just missing out on fun; they risk losing critical coping mechanisms that safeguard their mental health.

Dr. Brown's principles encourage adults to reintroduce themselves to the joy of play, urging them to rediscover activities that exhilarate them, make them lose track of time, or fill them with a childlike sense of wonder. Whether it's through sports, music, art, or even simple games, he advocates for play to be an unmissable fixture in the everyday routine.

Implementing Play in Adult Life

Knowing the importance of play is one thing but integrating it into the hectic schedule of adulthood is another. How can one possibly find time for play in between work deadlines, family responsibilities, and social commitments?

The key is to start small. It could be as simple as dancing while cooking, singing in the shower, joking with colleagues, or playing casual games with family. Technology today also allows various playful interactions, from digital games to interactive learning opportunities that one can engage with.

Another strategy is to include play in social interactions. Organise game nights, participate in community sports or join clubs with interests in playful activities. These not only provide a chance to play but also strengthen social bonds and create a support system.

Finally, don't overlook the role of play in problem-solving. Approaching challenges with a playful mindset can lead to creative solutions and make the process enjoyable rather than stressful. It's about changing the perspective from seeing play as a distraction to viewing it as a productivity booster.

As this chapter has explained, play is far from a childish indulgence. It's a sanctuary for the mind, a gym for our creative muscles, and a glue that fortifies social bonds. The research of experts like Magnuson, Barnett, Proyer, Guitard, Ferland, Dutil, Zhang, Li, and Dr. Stuart Brown converges on one critical point: play is indispensable for adults, not just for happiness but for health, well-being, and a fulfilling life.

In a society that often associates adulthood with seriousness and stresses productivity, supporting the idea of play may seem like a rebellious act. Yet, it's a rebellion worth embracing. As we allow ourselves the gift of play, we're not just granting ourselves a momentary escape. We're honouring our inherent human need for joy, creativity, and connection. So, go ahead, and give yourself permission to play. The benefits, as we've seen, are profound and all-encompassing, resonating through every facet of adult life.

Here is a practical guide, a table that breaks down the concept of play into accessible categories. It outlines various forms of playful activities and practical ways to weave them into the fabric of our daily routines. Whether you're seeking stress relief, intellectual stimulation, or a stronger social bond, there's a form of play just for you. Explore, engage, and most importantly, enjoy!

Type of play	Description	How to engage
Physical Play	Activities that engage the body, promoting health and stress relief.	Participate in sports, dance, hike, swim, or even engage in playful wrestling with your pet. Physical play isn't about the intensity; it's about having fun.
Creative Play	Expressing oneself through arts and crafts, storytelling, or other forms of artistic expression.	Paint, sculpt, write poetry or stories, engage in DIY home projects, or create music. Don't worry about the end product; enjoy the process.
Social Play	Interacting with others in enjoyable, cooperative, and competitive activities.	Organise game nights, join clubs, play team-based games, or engage in community events. Social play helps build relationships and communication skills.
Intellectual Play	Challenging the brain with puzzles, books, educational games, or discussions.	Solve puzzles, participate in trivia nights, read challenging books, or engage in deep discussions on interesting topics.
Imaginative Play	Engaging the imagination to create new worlds, scenarios, or solutions.	Daydream, role-play, think of new ideas or inventions or brainstorm different solutions to problems in a 'what-if' playful scenario.

> *"By understanding your own attachment history, you can break the cycle and build healthier, more secure relationships."*
> ~Dr. Sue Johnson~

Attachment Theory

Understanding the Bonds that Shape Us

Attachment Theory is a fascinating concept that helps us understand how we grow emotionally and connect with others throughout our lives. Imagine a baby and how it feels safe and calm when held by a loving parent. This simple yet profound bond is the foundation of Attachment Theory. It's all about the deep, lasting connections we form, starting from when we are very young.

This theory is vital because it helps us understand why we feel close to some people and distant from others. It shows us how our earliest relationships, especially with our caregivers, shape our feelings, thoughts and even how we deal with relationships as we grow up. It's like a blueprint for our emotional world, influencing how we make friends, how we act in relationships, and how we raise our own children.

Now, let's take a step back in time to see where these ideas came from. Attachment Theory was developed in the mid-20th century, a time when the relationships between parents and children were being studied more closely than ever before. The main architect behind this theory was a British psychologist named John Bowlby. He believed that the bonds children form with their parents or caregivers are crucial for survival. This was a groundbreaking idea because, before this, many people thought that children just needed physical care like food and shelter.

Bowlby's work led him to propose that children come into the world biologically pre-programmed to form attachments with others because this helps them survive. He suggested that these early relationships influence a person's feelings and behaviour all the way into adulthood.

But how did Bowlby come up with these ideas? He observed children and noticed how distressed they became when separated from their parents. He believed that this anxiety was a natural part of human development. But he didn't stop there. He also thought about how these patterns of attachment continued into adult life, affecting relationships and even parenting styles.

Mary Ainsworth, an American-Canadian psychologist who worked with Bowlby, took his ideas further by developing ways to study attachment between infants and their caregivers. One of her famous contributions is the "Strange Situation" procedure, a fascinating study that observed how babies reacted when they were temporarily separated from their mothers. Through this and other research, Ainsworth identified different "styles" of attachment, or ways that children bond with their caregivers.

Together, Bowlby and Ainsworth laid the groundwork for what we now understand about the emotional bonds that shape our lives. They showed us that the need to form strong, loving relationships is not just something nice to have but is essential to our well-being and survival. Their work has influenced decades of research and helped countless individuals understand themselves and their relationships better.

In this chapter, we'll dive deeper into these ideas, exploring how attachment theory explains the way we connect with others and how it influences our behaviour from infancy to adulthood. So, get ready to explore the invisible ties that bind us to the people we love and how these early experiences shape our journey through life.

Attachment Styles: Understanding How We Relate to Others

In Attachment Theory, psychologists have identified four main styles that describe how people typically think, feel, and behave in their relationships. These styles are like the patterns of connecting with others that we often develop from our earliest years.

Secure Attachment: If you're someone with a secure attachment, you strike a beautiful balance between getting close to others and maintaining your independence. This balance isn't just good for you; it's beneficial for the people in your life, too. You have the superpower of being a stable base for others, showing them what a secure relationship looks like. Your comfort with intimacy can encourage those around you to open up and trust more, creating a ripple effect of healthy relationships in your community.

Anxious Attachment: For those with an anxious attachment style, relationships can sometimes feel like a rollercoaster of emotions, filled with worries about how strong your connections really are. Recognising this pattern in yourself is the first step towards change. By learning to calm your own fears and clearly asking for what you need, you can transform your relationships into more stable and reassuring spaces. It's also a chance to understand that not every worry you have is a reflection of reality, helping you approach your relationships with a calmer, more grounded perspective.

Avoidant Attachment: If you resonate with an avoidant attachment style, you might value your independence above all else, sometimes at the expense of closeness with others. Understanding this about yourself is a powerful opportunity to gently stretch your boundaries. By allowing yourself small moments of vulnerability, you can discover that showing your true self is the key to deeper and more meaningful connections. This doesn't mean losing your independence; rather, it's about enriching your life with the strength that comes from real, heartfelt connections.

Disorganised Attachment: If you find yourself with a disorganised attachment style, your feelings about relationships can be pretty mixed up. You might long to be close to someone but feel nervous once you are. It's like wanting something but feeling unsure once you have it. This happens because your past experiences have left you with mixed messages about what to expect from people. Realising this about yourself is a big step forward. It helps you understand why you might feel this way and starts you on the path to better relationships. By getting to know your mixed feelings, you can begin to find a way to feel more comfortable with both getting close to people and having your own space. Learning about your disorganised attachment can help you move towards having relationships that make you feel safe and valued, allowing you to be yourself with others.

Critical Periods: The Formative Windows of Attachment

'Critical Periods' are like special chapters in the early years of a child's life when they are very open to the influences around them. In terms of attachment, this phase is usually considered to be the early years, from birth to around three years old. During these crucial years, having someone who consistently takes care of them and responds to their needs is incredibly important. This time acts as an opening for creating strong emotional connections that help the child grow in their feelings and how they get along with others.

These years are a golden chance for the child to form secure attachments, which are like invisible safety nets supporting their journey into the wider world. These attachments are not just about being physically close; they're about the child feeling understood and valued. When a child knows they can count on someone, they carry this trust into other relationships throughout their life.

However, if these secure attachments aren't developed during this critical period, it might be harder to build them later. While it's not impossible, it can take more effort and time. This is why the early years are so important – they set the foundation for how the child will connect with others as they grow. It's about giving the child the best start possible, filled with care and attention, to help them become confident and caring individuals.

However, attachment style can change over time because of different life events. Imagine you started off with a secure attachment because your caregivers were always there for you, making you feel safe and loved. But then, suppose something big happens in your life, like a major loss, a big move, or a relationship breakdown. These events can shake up your feelings and the way you see the world.

When big changes or challenges happen, you might start feeling more unsure about the people around you. You might worry more about whether they'll stick by you or if they really care. This shift can move you from feeling secure to feeling more anxious in your relationships. You might start needing more reassurance from people to feel okay, which is a sign of becoming more anxiously attached.

It's important to know that it's normal for your attachment style to evolve based on your experiences. Life can be unpredictable, and the way we react to things can change over time. But the good news is, just as your attachment style can change in response to tough times, it can also change for the better. With the right support, like talking to a trusted friend, a family member, or a professional like a therapist, you can work through your fears and start feeling more secure again.

In this context, the work of Dr. Sue Johnson, a prominent psychologist and developer of Emotionally Focused Therapy (EFT), is particularly relevant. She has shown that it's possible to move towards a more secure attachment style with understanding, effort, and the right kind of support. According to Dr. Johnson, engaging with our emotions and forming positive, trusting relationships can lead us back to feeling secure. So, even if recent events have left you feeling more anxious, there is a pathway to regaining a sense of stability and trust in your relationships.

Internal Working Models: The Blueprints of Relationships

Early attachments are not just about the relationships we have as children; they form "internal working models" that shape our expectations and behaviour in relationships throughout life. These are like internal blueprints or guidelines that we carry within us. They influence how we view ourselves, how we expect others to treat us, and how we interpret others' actions.

For example, if a child has caregivers who are responsive and consistently meet their needs, the child is likely to develop a working model of relationships where they see themselves as worthy of love and expect others to be kind and helpful. On the other hand, if a child's caregivers are distant or unpredictable, the child might grow up feeling unworthy of love or expect others to be untrustworthy or unavailable.

By understanding these attachment styles and underlying concepts, we can better understand ourselves and the people around us. It can help us recognise why we feel and behave the way we do in relationships and guide us towards healthier, more fulfilling connections.

Applying Attachment Theory to Enhance Our Relationships

Understanding Attachment Theory isn't just academic; it's a tool that can enrich our personal lives. By recognising our own attachment style and the styles of those around us, we can foster deeper connections and healthier relationships. Here's how we can use this knowledge practically:

1. Self-Reflection: Start by identifying your own attachment style. Are you secure, anxious, avoidant, or disorganised? Understanding this can help you become aware of your behaviours and needs in relationships. For example, if you know you have an anxious attachment style, you might recognise your need for reassurance and work on communicating this need to your partner in a calm manner.

2. Communicate Openly: Open and honest communication is the cornerstone of any strong relationship. Share your feelings, fears, and needs with your partner, friends, or family members. If you understand your attachment style, explain it to them. This can help them understand your perspective and respond better to your needs.

3. Respond Sensitively: Just as you have your own attachment style, so do the people around you. Pay attention to their cues and try to understand their needs. For instance, if someone close to you has an avoidant attachment style, they might value independence. Respecting their need for space while gently encouraging closeness can strengthen your bond.

4. Seek Consistency: People with secure attachments often had consistent and reliable caregivers. Try to be reliable and consistent in your relationships. If you promise to do something, follow through. This builds trust and security, laying the groundwork for a stable relationship.

5. Build Emotional Intelligence: This involves being aware of your emotions and those of others. By understanding and managing your feelings, you can interact with others in a more empathetic and understanding way. This is particularly beneficial in managing conflicts and maintaining strong relationships.

6. Professional Guidance: If you find that your attachment style is significantly impacting your relationships, consider seeking help from a therapist or counsellor. They can offer strategies and support to help you understand your attachment style and work towards forming healthier relationships.

7. Practice Patience and Compassion: Change doesn't happen overnight. Be patient with yourself and others as you work through these changes. Remember, everyone comes with their own history and set of experiences that shape their attachment style.

8. Create New Experiences: Positive experiences can help build secure attachments. Plan activities or create rituals that help you and your loved ones feel connected and valued. This could be as simple as a weekly dinner date, a nightly chat, or a regular family game night.

By applying the principles of Attachment Theory in these practical ways, we can move towards healthier, more fulfilling relationships. Remember, understanding and compassion are key. As we grow in our understanding of ourselves and others, we pave the way for deeper connections and a richer, more compassionate life.

Wrapping up our journey into Attachment Theory, we've gained new insights into how deep emotional bonds influence us from a young age. We started with the simple yet profound connection between a parent and child and moved through the complex emotions that play out in our adult relationships. Thanks to experts like John Bowlby, Mary Ainsworth and Dr. Sue Johnson, we now understand the silent strings that connect our past with our present.

We've looked at different ways people bond, like secure, anxious, avoidant, and disorganised styles, and realised how these early patterns affect our connections today. It's clear now that our first relationships shape how we interact with people later in life.

But understanding this is just the start. Using what we've learned from Attachment Theory can really change our relationships for the better. Recognising our own style of bonding and understanding others can lead to stronger, more meaningful relationships. By talking openly, staying consistent, understanding our emotions, and creating new positive experiences, we can improve the way we connect with others.

So, let's take these valuable lessons with us. Let's be patient and kind with ourselves and those around us as we work on building better, stronger relationships. Here's to moving forward with a better understanding of ourselves and the people we care about, aiming for a life filled with deeper connections and more love.

Attachment Style Self-Test

This self-test is designed to help you identify your predominant attachment style based on your typical behaviours and feelings in close relationships. The main attachment styles are Secure, Avoidant, Anxious, and Disorganised. Understanding your attachment style can provide valuable insights into how you relate to others and guide you toward healthier relationships.

Instructions:
Read each statement and decide how much it applies to you in romantic relationships. Answer honestly for the most accurate assessment.

Rate each statement using the following scale:

5 - Very much like me
4 - Mostly like me
3 - Somewhat like me
2 - Not much like me
1 - Not like me at all

1. I often worry that my partner doesn't really love me or won't want to stay with I need a lot of reassurance that I am loved by my partner.me.	
2. I prefer not to get too close to others.	
3. I am comfortable depending on others and having others depend on me.	
4. I often feel uncomfortable when someone wants to be very close to me.	
5. I worry a lot about being abandoned.	
6. I am very comfortable sharing my feelings, thoughts, and needs with my partner.	
7. I prefer not to show others how I feel deep down.	
8. My partner often wants me to be more intimate than I am comfortable with.	
9. I find others are reluctant to get as close as I would like.	
10. When I show my feelings for others, I'm afraid they will not feel the same about me.	
11. I find it relatively easy to get close to others.	
12. I sometimes feel that I force my partners to show more feeling and closeness than they are comfortable with.	
13. I feel uneasy when a romantic partner wants to get closer than I am comfortable with.	

Scoring:

Add up your scores for the following groups of statements to determine your predominant attachment style:

Secure Attachment: Statements 3, 6, 11. Maximum score: 15 points.

Anxious Attachment: Statements 1, 5, 9, 12. Maximum score: 20 points.

Avoidant Attachment: Statements 2, 4, 7, 8, 10, 13. Maximum score: 30 points.

Results:

Secure Attachment (11-15 points): Comfortable with intimacy and typically warm and loving.

Anxious Attachment (16-20 points): Often worried about relationships and abandonment, desiring closeness and reassurance.

Avoidant Attachment (21-30 points): Values independence, often uncomfortable with closeness and intimacy.

This self-test is a starting point for understanding how you relate to others. Attachment styles can change over time with self-awareness and personal development. If you're interested in exploring your attachment style further, consider seeking feedback from a therapist or reading more about attachment theory.

This self-test is a starting point for understanding your attachment style. It's important to remember that attachment styles can change over time with self-awareness and effort. If you're interested in exploring your attachment style further, consider seeking feedback from a therapist or reading more about attachment theory.

"The reality is that you will grieve forever. You will not 'get over' the loss of a loved one; you will learn to live with it. You will heal and you will rebuild yourself around the loss you have suffered."

~Elisabeth Kübler-Ross~

The Grief Puzzle

Grief isn't just a quick, passing sadness that only shows up when someone we love passes away. Oh no, it's much bigger than that. Grief is like a deep change that happens inside us, touching every part of who we are. It's not just about saying goodbye to a person; it can come from losing all sorts of things that matter to us—like our jobs, our relationships, the dreams we've held onto, or even just facing big changes that we didn't see coming.

Grief is something that everyone goes through at some point, even though it comes from different situations for each person.

Despite these different causes, grief consistently leads to a change in us. It's a part of life that shows how deeply we feel and connect, and while it can be really tough, it also helps us learn about ourselves and grow.

From a physiological standpoint, grief's first move is to cue the stress hormones. Elevations in cortisol can be noted, subtly pushing the balance in our internal environment. This might lead to disrupted sleep patterns, a frequent companion of grief, making nights longer and days heavier. Our immune responses might dip, making us more susceptible to infections. There's also a marked change in appetite for many; food might lose its appeal or, conversely, become a temporary refuge.

The heart, always rhythmic and constant, doesn't escape grief's touch either. Some report palpitations or a heightened sense of awareness of their heartbeats, like a soft drum echoing the loss. Blood pressure can be unpredictable, and in extreme cases, there's even a condition known as "broken heart syndrome", where the heart temporarily mimics symptoms of a heart attack, showcasing the profound connection between our emotions and our physiological responses.

As Kübler-Ross highlighted, grief comes with a range of emotions. The most obvious is deep sadness, which many people associate with grief. However, there are other feelings that are just as important. Anger, for instance, can emerge, sometimes turning inward, other times lashing out. There are also feelings of guilt and regret, which can haunt us with endless "what ifs" about past actions and decisions. Amidst these intense emotions, there are also moments of numbness, offering a temporary escape from the emotional turmoil.

In the tumultuous journey of grief, it is important to remember that emotions do not follow a linear path. Glimmers of acceptance and understanding may emerge, only to be overshadowed by anger or guilt. Grief is a complex dance, with emotions ebbing and flowing, circling back, and overlapping. Despite these fluctuations, over time, even the most vast and varied emotions begin to align toward healing.

It is essential to recognise all manifestations of grief, both physiological and emotional, as natural responses to loss. Even when they return unexpectedly, acknowledging these feelings is the first step to navigating the maze of grief and emerging with a deeper understanding of ourselves.

Mourning
Mourning is a unique experience for everyone, like a personal journey where each person finds their own way to cope and heal from loss. People discover different methods and strategies that touch their hearts and help them in this process. Mourning is a critical step in healing from loss, and there are many well-known methods that people find helpful.

The initial steps into mourning involve honouring the void. This is not about immediate acceptance, but rather a space to breathe and to recognise the profoundness of the absence. By externalising this recognition, whether through rituals, memories, or simple acknowledgment, we start our journey towards acceptance. This honouring is essential, acting as the foundation upon which the healing journey builds.

As the journey progresses, emotions, often tumultuous and conflicting, come to the forefront. These feelings are not mere disturbances; they are intricate messages from the psyche. To navigate this emotional labyrinth, mourning offers the gift of introspection. It is a realm where feelings are not invaders, but rather visitors, each one bringing its own insight and lesson. By embracing these emotions in the sanctuary of mourning, healing finds its subtle, nurturing rhythm.

Humans are naturally social beings, and there's something deeply moving about sharing grief with others. When people come together in their sorrow, it forms a network of support. This network is built from shared stories, tears, and memories, offering comfort through empathy and understanding. In sharing grief, people find not only comfort but also the reassurance that they are not alone in their pain. This shared experience is a powerful reminder of the strength found in togetherness during tough times.

Loss is an event, but finding meaning is the journey that follows. When we face loss, we are often disoriented and seeking guidance. The quest to find meaning is not about replacing what was lost, but rather about finding a new perspective in the changed landscape of our lives.

Dr. Viktor Frankl, a Jewish psychiatrist and neurologist, survived the Holocaust. In his book, Man's Search for Meaning, Frankl describes his ordeal in the concentration camps and how he found meaning in his suffering. He believed that humans are primarily driven by a "will to meaning," and that even in the darkest of circumstances, we can find meaning in our lives.

The journey of uncovering meaning after loss is an active engagement. We must ask ourselves questions such as: What can this experience teach me? How has this loss reshaped my understanding of life, relationships, or myself? Delving into these inquiries can offer insights and highlight values or priorities that we may have overlooked before.

Finding meaning is not a solitary pursuit. Engaging with others, sharing narratives of loss, and listening to diverse experiences can illuminate shared human truths. Communities, such as support groups, spiritual congregations, or simply circles of friends, offer collective wisdom. In these shared spaces, individual narratives weave into the larger tapestry, enriching the collective understanding of loss and recovery.

Ultimately, the quest to derive meaning from loss is not about arriving at a destination. It is a continuous process of evolution, reflection, and growth. The scars of loss might remain, but the stories we etch around them, the meanings we derive, and the paths we chart, ensure that these scars become testament to resilience, depth, and the ever-evolving narrative of life.

Dr. Frankl's ordeal and his subsequent writings on finding meaning in suffering offer a powerful source of inspiration for those who are grieving. He reminds us that even in the depths of despair, there is always hope. And that even the most painful experiences can teach us and help us to grow.

As we navigate the journey of finding meaning after loss, let us keep Dr. Frankl's words in mind:

"Everything can be taken from a man but one thing: the last of the human freedoms—to choose one's attitude in any given set of circumstances, to choose one's own way."

As we wrap up this chapter about dealing with grief, let's hold onto a powerful idea from Dr. Edith Eva Eger, an Auschwitz survivor and renowned psychologist. – She emphasises that while we cannot control our circumstances, we always have a choice in how we respond to them. This is a central theme in her book "The Choice," where she reflects on her experiences in Auschwitz and how she learned that our most significant freedom is the ability to choose our attitude in any given set of circumstances.

"Trauma is personal. It does not disappear if it is not validated. When it is ignored or invalidated, the silent screams continue internally heard only by the one held captive. When someone enters the pain and hears the screams, healing can begin." –

~Dr. Danielle Legg~

Trauma: The Unseen Scars Within

Let's embark on a journey into the human mind and heart. It's a trip that will help us understand trauma, how it affects us, and how we can heal. But before we begin, let's take a moment to appreciate the immense strength and resilience that we, as humans, possess. Every experience, be it delightful or distressing, shapes us. And sometimes, the distressing ones leave lasting imprints on our minds and bodies. That's what we call trauma.

Dr. Bessel van der Kolk, a prominent trauma expert, investigates deep into the realm of trauma in his groundbreaking book "The Body Keeps the Score." He combines decades of research, clinical experience, and real-life stories to shed light on how trauma changes the brain and body, and how one can recover and regain control. Let's uncover some of these insights.

Trauma: More Than Just Memories

Many believe that trauma resides in the memories of terrible events. While that's partially true, trauma is more than just a memory. It's an experience that gets under our skin, affecting our brain, our emotions, and even our physical body. Think of trauma as a heavy backpack filled with bricks. You can't just put it down; it's there, weighing you down, affecting every step you take.

The impact of trauma can lead to sleepless nights, flashbacks, anxiety, and sometimes a deep sense of disconnect from the world. People who've experienced trauma might find it hard to trust others or even feel safe. This isn't because they are weak, but because their brain and body are trying to protect them from further harm.

The Brain's Response: Fight, Flight, or Freeze

Our brains are brilliant. They're designed to protect us from harm. When faced with danger, our brain activates the fight, flight, or freeze response. This is our brain's way of deciding whether we should confront the threat, run away from it, or stay still and hope it passes.

For instance, imagine walking in a forest and suddenly spotting a snake. Your heart races, your pupils dilate, and without even thinking, you might jump back or freeze. That's your brain taking charge. Now, for someone who has experienced trauma, the snake might not be a physical entity. It could be a loud noise, a touch, or even a memory that triggers this intense response.

How Trauma Sticks Around

The tricky part is that trauma, especially when it's repeated or prolonged, can change the very structure and function of the brain. The brain's alarm system, the amygdala, becomes hyperactive. The prefrontal cortex, responsible for rational thinking and decision-making, gets suppressed. This means that even when there's no real threat, the brain might perceive danger.

When a person experiences trauma, it can have a significant impact on their mental state. Trauma can affect how the brain functions, often leading to difficulties in processing emotions, thoughts, and reactions. This disruption can make it harder for a person to feel comfortable or at ease, as they might struggle with distressing memories or feelings. However, it's important to understand that recovery from trauma is possible. Through various therapeutic approaches, support systems, and personal coping strategies, individuals can work towards healing. This process involves addressing and managing the effects of trauma, restoring a sense of control and well-being over time.

The Body's Role

As Dr. van der Kolk highlights, our bodies keep the score. The trauma doesn't just reside in our minds; it's felt in our bodies too. People with trauma might experience unexplained aches, tension, and even illnesses. It's as if the body is echoing the distress the mind feels.

There's also a deep connection between trauma and our ability to feel present in our bodies. Some people might feel detached, as if they're floating, while others might be hyper-aware of every sensation. The key takeaway is that healing from trauma isn't just about addressing the mind; it's about listening to and caring for the body too.

One of the most insidious ways trauma infiltrates the body is through the relentless drip of chronic stress. Visualise it as a faucet that refuses to stop dripping - an incessant, maddening sound that resonates within your body.

Dr. Bessel van der Kolk, a leading authority on trauma, has explored the relationship between trauma and chronic stress extensively. His research, along with numerous scientific studies, paints a vivid picture of how traumatic experiences can disrupt the body's stress response.

Imagine you're in a state of perpetual alertness, your nervous system constantly on edge. This is how chronic stress operates within the body of a trauma survivor. Your stress hormones, like cortisol, surge continually, akin to water overflowing from a relentlessly dripping faucet.

As time goes by, constant stress can really wear you down. This ongoing tension can start causing physical health issues. High blood pressure can become a real risk because your body is always in a heightened state of alert. Digestive problems might also start to show up, a direct result of the body's continuous stress response.

Trauma does not stop at hijacking your stress response; it also weakens your body's defences. Envision your immune system as a vigilant guardian, protecting you from external threats. However, trauma compromises this guardian, leaving you vulnerable to illness.

Dr. Bessel van der Kolk's research highlights how trauma can affect the immune system, making people more likely to get sick. Trauma impacts the body in such a way that it becomes less effective at fighting off diseases. Studies have shown that experiencing trauma can lead to a weaker immune system. This means that someone who has experienced trauma might find themselves catching infections and getting ill more easily than before, as their body's natural defense system isn't as strong as it used to be.

Now, consider your sleep as a crucial component of your body's healing process. It is during these hours of rest that your body repairs and recharges itself, regaining balance and energy for the next day.

Dr. Bessel van der Kolk's research has delved into the relationship between trauma and sleep disturbances. He and his colleagues have observed how trauma disrupts the natural sleep cycle, leading to restlessness, nightmares, and difficulty finding solace in the stillness of the night.

This disturbed sleep isn't just a minor inconvenience. It's a profound disruption that can lead to chronic fatigue, a fog that obscures your mobile's delicate balance. Deprived of its necessary rest, your body finds it difficult to restore its natural state of equilibrium.

Finally, let's delve into how trauma alters your perception of pain. Your body's pain threshold is a finely tuned instrument, capable of discerning between discomfort and agony. Trauma, however, distorts this instrument, making you more sensitive to discomfort.

Dr. Bessel van der Kolk's research has also explored the links between trauma and altered pain perception. Trauma survivors often find themselves more sensitive to physical discomfort, with minor aches feeling like major ordeals. It's as if your body's volume knob has been turned up, amplifying every sensation.

It's the result of trauma's pervasive impact, making even the subtlest disturbances resonate with intensity.
Trauma is not just a battle fought in the mind; it's a pervasive force that disrupts the delicate balance of the body. Chronic stress, weakened immunity, sleep disturbances, and altered pain perception are all part of the collateral damage inflicted by trauma. It's like a mobile, once gracefully swaying in the breeze, now thrown into disarray. Understanding these physical consequences is crucial, for it underscores the urgency of addressing trauma's far-reaching effects on the entire self, as illuminated by the extensive research of Dr. Bessel van der Kolk and other scientists in the field.

The Emotional Rollercoaster

Now, let's delve into emotions. Imagine emotions as a seesaw in a playground. On one side, you have positive emotions like joy, love, and contentment, while on the other, you have negative ones like fear, anger, and sadness. Trauma tilts this seesaw heavily towards negativity, making it hard to find happiness and peace.

It's not just about feeling bad; it's also about how we cope. Trauma often leads to unhealthy coping mechanisms, such as substance abuse or self-harm, as we try to numb the pain or regain control.

So, we've unravelled the enigma of trauma. It's more than just emotional; it affects the brain, body, and emotions in profound ways. But how can we heal? This is where Bessel van der Kolk and his pioneering work come into play.

"The Body Keeps the Score"

Van der Kolk's magnum opus, "The Body Keeps the Score," has become a cornerstone in the trauma field. Picture your body as a living diary, chronicling every traumatic event you've ever experienced. Even when your conscious mind tries to forget, your body remembers. Van der Kolk delves into how trauma resides within our bodies, influencing thoughts, behaviours, and physical health.

One pivotal concept is "dysregulation," the idea that trauma throws our body systems out of balance. Dysregulation can manifest as anxiety, depression, chronic pain, and a slew of other symptoms. Van der Kolk emphasises addressing these physical and emotional aspects in therapy.

Yoga and Mindfulness as Healing Tools

Van der Kolk's exploration of yoga and mindfulness practices for trauma survivors is another groundbreaking facet of his work. Picture yoga as a gentle, rhythmic dance that helps your body release pent-up tension. These practices encourage individuals to reconnect with their bodies and the present moment, often lost in the trauma's chaos.

Research conducted by van der Kolk and his colleagues has shown that yoga and mindfulness can effectively reduce PTSD symptoms and enhance emotional regulation. It's like finding a serene oasis in the midst of trauma's desert.

EMDR – Rewriting Trauma Narratives

Now that we've glimpsed the science of trauma and Dr. Bessel van der Kolk's groundbreaking research, let's journey into the transformative therapy known as Eye Movement Desensitisation and Reprocessing (EMDR)

Imagine you're quickly scanning the environment, like when you're trying to find someone in a crowded place, and your eyes are moving fast from face to face. Now, think about the idea that this kind of quick eye movement could actually help you heal from really tough, painful memories. It might sound like something from a science fiction story, but it's a real thing. This method is called EMDR, which stands for Eye Movement Desensitisation and Reprocessing. It's a therapy technique used to help people overcome the stress from past traumatic experiences.

EMDR stands for Eye Movement Desensitisation and Reprocessing. Quite a mouthful, I know! But don't let the jargon intimidate you. At its heart, EMDR is a therapeutic technique that helps people heal from traumatic events in their lives.

The Backstory
In the late 1980s, and Dr. Francine Shapiro is taking a walk in the park. She's engrossed in her thoughts, some of which are rather distressing. But she notices something peculiar. As her eyes move back and forth, those distressing thoughts seem to lose their sting. Intrigued, Dr. Shapiro dives deep into research and, voila, EMDR is born!

How Does EMDR Work?

Now, this is where it gets interesting. Imagine your brain as a sophisticated computer system. Sometimes, when something traumatic happens, the memory of that event gets stuck, like a glitch. Every time you think of that memory, you feel the same intense emotions you felt during the actual event.

EMDR aims to "unstuck" these memories. By making you recall the distressing memory and simultaneously guiding your eyes to move in a specific pattern, the brain starts reprocessing the memory. Over time, the intensity of the emotion linked to that memory fades.

Scientific Validation of EMDR
EMDR is not just a whimsical concept; it's backed by scientific evidence. Numerous studies have shown its effectiveness in reducing PTSD symptoms and helping individuals recover from traumatic experiences.

These are just a few of the many scientific studies that have been conducted on EMDR. The research consistently shows that EMDR is an effective treatment for PTSD and other trauma-related disorders.

- "Eye Movement Desensitisation and Reprocessing (EMDR): A Meta-Analysis of Treatment Outcomes" by Davidson et al. (2006) found that EMDR was effective in reducing symptoms of post-traumatic stress disorder (PTSD) in adults. The study reviewed 14 randomised controlled trials and found that EMDR was more effective than other treatments, such as cognitive behavioural therapy (CBT), in reducing PTSD symptoms.

- "A Meta-Analysis of Randomised Controlled Studies of Eye Movement Desensitisation and Reprocessing for PTSD" by Bradley et al. (2005) found that EMDR was effective in reducing symptoms of PTSD in adults and children. The study reviewed 12 randomised controlled trials and found that EMDR was more effective than other treatments, such as supportive counselling, in reducing PTSD symptoms.

- "Eye Movement Desensitisation and Reprocessing (EMDR) for the Treatment of Posttraumatic Stress Disorder: A Meta-Analysis" by van Etten and Taylor (2000) found that EMDR was effective in reducing symptoms of PTSD in adults. The study reviewed 8 randomised controlled trials and found that EMDR was more effective than other treatments, such as exposure therapy, in reducing PTSD symptoms.

- "Eye Movement Desensitisation and Reprocessing (EMDR): A Review of Controlled Studies" by Shapiro (1995) found that EMDR was effective in reducing symptoms of PTSD in adults. The study reviewed 12 controlled trials and found that EMDR was more effective than other treatments, such as supportive counselling, in reducing PTSD symptoms.

- "A Randomised Controlled Trial of Eye Movement Desensitisation and Reprocessing for Posttraumatic Stress Disorder" by Marcus et al. (2006) found that EMDR was effective in reducing symptoms of PTSD in adults. The study randomly assigned participants to EMDR or supportive counselling and found that EMDR was more effective in reducing PTSD symptoms.

In addition to the studies mentioned above, there have been many other studies that have investigated the effectiveness of EMDR for a variety of other conditions, including anxiety disorders, depression, pain, and phobias. The results of these studies have been mixed, but overall, they suggest that EMDR may be an effective treatment for a range of mental health problems.

It is important to note that EMDR is not a cure-all. It is a therapy that can help people to process traumatic experiences and reduce the symptoms of PTSD and other trauma-related disorders. However, it is not a guarantee that everyone will benefit from EMDR.

Here are some notable organisations that have endorsed or supported EMDR therapy:

- World Health Organisation (WHO): The World Health Organisation recognises EMDR as an evidence-based treatment for post-traumatic stress disorder (PTSD) in its guidelines for the management of conditions specifically related to stress.
- American Psychological Association (APA): The APA acknowledges EMDR as one of the effective treatments for

trauma-related conditions, including PTSD, in their clinical practice guidelines.

- U.S. Department of Veterans Affairs (VA): The VA's National Centre for PTSD includes EMDR as one of the recommended treatments for PTSD. It is among the therapies offered to veterans and active-duty
- service members.
- National Institute for Health and Care Excellence (NICE - UK): NICE guidelines in the United Kingdom recommend EMDR as one of the treatments for PTSD. They emphasise the importance of offering evidence-based therapies like EMDR.
- International Society for Traumatic Stress Studies (ISTSS): ISTSS recognises EMDR as an effective treatment for PTSD and related trauma disorders. They provide resources and support for trauma professionals, including EMDR therapists.
- Substance Abuse and Mental Health Services Administration (SAMHSA): SAMHSA, a U.S. government agency, includes EMDR in its list of evidence-based practices for the treatment of trauma-related disorders.
- European Society for Traumatic Stress Studies (ESTSS): ESTSS acknowledges EMDR as a valid treatment option for trauma-related disorders and promotes its use among mental health professionals in Europe.
- Australian Psychological Society (APS): The APS includes EMDR among the evidence-based therapies recommended for PTSD and trauma-related conditions in their guidelines for psychologists.

These organisations have recognised EMDR based on research and clinical evidence, and they support its use as a therapeutic approach for individuals experiencing trauma-related symptoms. However, it's important to note that while EMDR is widely accepted and supported, individual treatment decisions should always be made in consultation with a qualified mental health professional who can assess the specific needs of each client or patient.

IMPORTANT: EMDR is not a therapy one can undertake casually. It requires trained and certified professionals. Typically, EMDR therapists have advanced degrees in psychology or counselling and undergo rigorous training in EMDR techniques. To ensure you're in capable hands, seek out therapists who are licensed in your region and hold certification from the EMDR International Association (EMDRIA).

The Art of Healing

Trauma can deeply affect our lives, but it doesn't have to shape everything about us. Dr. Bessel van der Kolk has conducted significant research demonstrating how we can recover from trauma. Therapies like EMDR are crucial in this recovery process. They help us incorporate our difficult experiences into a story of becoming stronger, learning, and developing resilience. This approach to recovery demonstrates that, even in the aftermath of trauma, we can grow and discover strength in our experiences.

The science behind trauma, as unveiled by van der Kolk, reminds us that trauma is not a life sentence but a journey we can navigate with purpose. Through reprocessing, reconnecting, and mastering our emotions, we have the power to reclaim our lives.

Even though trauma can deeply impact us, finding the right support and methods can guide us toward a path of hope and healing. This approach involves understanding and working through our traumatic experiences, transforming them into a narrative of resilience and recovery. It's about recognising the impact of our past and actively working to create a future where those experiences inform a journey of growth and strength, demonstrating that healing and moving forward are indeed possible.

Remember that healing is an art, a journey, and a testament to the strength of the human spirit.

> "The echo of our ancestors' pain resounds in our lives, calling us to look back and understand, in order to move forward and heal."
> ~Unknown~

Transgenerational Trauma

Transgenerational trauma, a term that has gained attention in recent years, refers to the transmission of traumatic experiences from one generation to the next. Imagine a shadow cast by a family's past hardships, affecting the emotions, thoughts, and behaviours of future generations. This trauma is not always visible and can be deeply embedded in the family's emotional DNA, influencing individuals without them even realising it.

To understand transgenerational trauma, we must look back at history. Consider the Holocaust, an event of immense suffering and loss. Survivors carried with them not just physical scars but deep psychological wounds. These wounds, in turn, affected their children and grandchildren, impacting their view of the world and themselves.

Similarly, the legacies of slavery, colonialism, and the trauma experienced by indigenous populations in residential schools are not confined to those who directly experienced these atrocities. The ripple effects of these historical injustices are seen in subsequent generations, manifesting as anxiety, distrust, and various other psychological effects. These examples serve to show how trauma can transcend time, affecting individuals decades after the original events occurred.

Understanding transgenerational trauma is crucial in today's society as it helps us comprehend the root causes of certain behaviours and emotional states in communities. Recognising this form of trauma is the first step towards healing and breaking the cycle of pain. It enables mental health professionals, educators, and policymakers to develop more effective support systems and interventions. Moreover, it fosters empathy and understanding among individuals, encouraging a more compassionate and inclusive community.

By acknowledging the enduring impact of past traumas, we can better support those affected and work towards a future where the chains of historical pain are broken. This understanding is not just about acknowledging the past; it's about shaping a more understanding and supportive future.

Biological insights, especially from epigenetics, reveal how trauma can impact families across generations. Epigenetics explores changes in gene expression, meaning how genes are switched on or off by different experiences. While our DNA remains constant, traumatic experiences can modify how this DNA operates within our bodies. These modifications can affect how we cope with stress and may be passed to the next generation, making them potentially more vulnerable to stress and trauma.

Dr. Rachel Yehuda, a leading researcher in this area, has made significant strides in understanding how these biological changes can be inherited, particularly in her work with Holocaust survivors and their children. She has identified that these groups can exhibit altered levels of cortisol, a stress hormone, suggesting a biological shift inherited from parent to child due to the trauma faced by the first generation.

Also, animal studies, particularly with mice, have provided concrete examples of how trauma can be passed down. Researchers, including Dr. Brian Dias from Emory University, conducted experiments showing that mice trained to associate a specific scent with a shock later showed fear when exposed to that scent, which is expected. However, what's remarkable is that their offspring, who were never exposed to the shock, also showed fear when they encountered the same scent. This suggests that the trauma experienced by the parent mice was somehow transmitted to their children, providing a clear model of how traumatic responses and memories can be inherited biologically.

These findings from both human and animal studies offer powerful evidence for the concept of transgenerational trauma. They illustrate the profound connection between our life experiences, particularly traumatic ones, and the biological changes they can trigger, changes that can be passed down through generations. This research highlights the intricate relationship between our biology and what we go through. It shows how deep trauma can impact not only the people who directly face it but also their future generations.

Transgenerational trauma isn't just a family issue; it's also about the bigger picture, including our culture and society. The stories we hear and tell in our culture and the way our society is built can keep trauma going from one generation to the next. Big unfair events in history, like colonialism, slavery, and racism, create situations that keep harming people. These situations often leave out certain groups from having good chances for work, community, and feeling well, which keeps the cycle of trauma going.

Also, the stories that our societies share about themselves and their past can shape how we remember and deal with trauma. If these stories leave out or get wrong the painful events, it stops people from healing and helps keep the trauma going in families.

Understanding these ideas helps us see the many ways trauma is passed down through generations. It's not only about what happens to individuals but also about how these personal experiences fit into bigger family, biological, and social settings. Knowing all this is really important for finding good ways to help people heal and stop the cycle of trauma.

Symptoms and How they Manifest

Feelings and Thoughts:
Trauma that is passed down through generations can deeply impact emotions. Dr. Rachel Yehuda's work sheds light on how individuals can inherit feelings such as anxiety and depression, leading them to experience excessive worry or profound sadness without any obvious reasons. They may also suffer from PTSD, finding themselves haunted by fears linked to traumas they never directly experienced. Dr. Yehuda's research suggests

these intense emotions might originate from traumatic events encountered by previous generations, impacting individuals today even though they were not present.

Behaviour Patterns:
This concealed pain can influence people's behaviours as well, as highlighted by Dr. Yehuda's findings. Some individuals may resort to drinking excessively or using drugs in an attempt to numb the inherited anguish. Others might avoid places, people, or situations that unknowingly remind them of their family's past traumas, or they may find it challenging to maintain healthy relationships, burdened by historical grievances. Dr. Yehuda indicates that such behaviours could be linked to trauma embedded in the family's past, affecting current actions without a clear understanding of the underlying reasons.

Cultural and Community Impact:
Dr. Yehuda's insights also demonstrate how trauma impacts entire communities. The collective memory, including traditions, stories, and beliefs, can bear the imprints of historical traumas. This means that the way a community conducts itself and its worldview may reflect the lingering effects of past adversities, passed through generations. Recognising this helps us comprehend that our community's behaviours and beliefs might be influenced by shared past traumas, shaping our collective attitudes and actions today.

Acknowledging these signs and behaviours, according to Dr. Yehuda's research, is vital. It helps us identify the origins of our feelings and behaviours, fostering better support and understanding for ourselves and one another. It's about promoting an environment where inherited traumas can be openly discussed and addressed, recognising that this is not an isolated struggle but a collective one.

Healing from Transgenerational Trauma

Talking About It:
Chatting about your feelings can be really helpful for your heart and mind. Look for someone kind and patient, someone who gives you space to speak without jumping in with their own thoughts straight away. This person could be a good mate, someone from your family, or another person you feel safe around. Remember, you don't need to spill everything at once. Just starting with small bits about how your day went or what's been on your mind can make a big difference.

If you're struggling to start the conversation, you could begin with something simple like, "Lately, I've been feeling a bit low and I'm not quite sure what's bothering me." This can open the door to more talks in the future. By sharing your thoughts, you might start to feel a bit lighter, as if you're not carrying all your worries alone. It's like when you share a heavy bag with someone; suddenly it's not so tough to carry.

When you open up, it can make you feel more connected and understood. It's not always easy to talk about tough stuff, but finding the right person who listens and understands can make a huge difference. They don't need to fix your problems – just being there, listening, and showing they care can make you feel supported and a bit less on your own with your troubles.

Understanding Your Family's History:
Exploring your family's past can be like uncovering a hidden treasure of stories and experiences. It's all about getting to know

where you come from and the journey of your ancestors. Sometimes, our families have gone through tough times or big challenges, like wars, moving to new places, or other hard situations. Knowing about these parts of your family's history can help you understand more about why you feel or act the way you do today.

You can start by chatting with older relatives. Ask them to share stories from their youth or tales they heard from their own parents and grandparents. These conversations can be eye-opening and can make you feel more connected to your family. If talking isn't an option, you might find old letters, photos, or even local history books that tell more about the time and place your family comes from.

When you learn about the hardships and triumphs your ancestors faced, you might find new respect and understanding for them—and for yourself. For example, if your grandmother lived through tough times and you see some of her strength in you, it might explain your own resilience in difficult situations.

Realising that your family's past experiences can shape your current emotions and behaviour can be enlightening. It might help you understand why certain things make you anxious or why you react a certain way in specific situations. This doesn't mean you are stuck with these feelings or actions, but understanding where they come from is the first step in dealing with them more effectively. It can change the way you see your personal challenges, making them feel less like personal failures and more like part of a larger story.

Learning Healthy Ways to Cope:
Finding positive ways to manage stress and emotions is key. This could include physical activities like walking or yoga, which help clear your mind and lower stress. Creative activities like drawing, writing, or making music can also help you express your feelings and thoughts. Even simple actions like deep breathing or meditating for a few minutes each day can make a big difference in how you feel.

Joining a Support Group:
You're not alone in this. Many people are dealing with similar feelings and situations. Joining a group where you can talk with others who understand what you're going through can be really helpful. You can share your own experiences and listen to others. This can be done through community centres, online forums, or mental health organisations. Hearing others' stories and sharing your own can be a strong reminder that you're not alone in this journey.

Seeking Professional Help:
Sometimes, the trauma is too much to handle by yourself, and that's completely okay. Therapists or counsellors are trained to help people deal with deep-seated issues. They can offer you new ways to think about what you're experiencing and suggest strategies to cope. There's no shame in asking for help; it's a sign of strength to know when you need support.

Connecting with Your Culture:
Your cultural heritage can be a source of strength and pride. Learning about your family's cultural background, traditions, and languages can help you feel a stronger connection to your ancestors and your own identity. You might want to try cooking traditional dishes, participating in cultural ceremonies, or

learning about the history of your people. This connection can offer comfort and a sense of belonging.

Healing is a personal journey that takes time, and it's different for everyone. It's okay to go at your own pace. Remember to be gentle with yourself, and recognise each small step you take towards healing.

Here are some gentle questions to ponder and write down in your journal or write here. These questions help you think about not just your family, but also the community and culture you're part of. Take it easy, and remember, this is about exploring your own experiences and those around you:

1. What are some patterns or behaviours I've noticed in my family, and do I see these in our wider community or cultural group?

_____
_____
_____
_____
_____
_____

2. How do my personal feelings and actions mirror those of my family members, community, or cultural background?

_____
_____
_____
_____
_____
_____

3. Have I felt fears or anxieties that I can't link directly to my own experiences, but that might relate to my family's, community's, or culture's past?

_____
_____
_____
_____
_____
_____

4. In what ways have the historical events that affected my ancestors shaped not only my family's but also my community's or culture's beliefs and behaviours?

_____
_____
_____
_____
_____
_____

5. What coping strategies or ways of dealing with problems have been passed down in my family? How are these viewed or practised in my wider community or culture?

_____
_____
_____
_____
_____
_____

6. Do I react strongly to certain situations, and can I see a connection between these reactions and my family's, community's, or culture's history?

___

7. How have the traumatic experiences of my ancestors influenced my own views on trust, safety, and relationships within both my family and community?

___

8. Are there any traditions, stories, or silent rules in my family that reflect broader cultural or community practices, possibly stemming from past traumas?

___

9. How could healing from generational traumas change not only my life but also impact my family, community, and cultural group?

_____
_____
_____
_____
_____
_____

10. Have I or others in my community tried to uncover or heal from issues that we think come from our past? What did we find, and how did it make us feel?

_____
_____
_____
_____
_____
_____

Remember, these questions are for you to explore your thoughts and feelings about your family, community, and culture. Writing them down can help you understand yourself and your world a bit better.

Epilogue

As we turn the final pages of this journey, it's essential to recognise that the path of self-discovery doesn't end here. Each step you've taken while navigating these chapters is a testament to your commitment to personal growth and a reminder that the quest for inner peace and understanding is an ongoing journey.

Remember, the insights and strategies shared within these pages are tools — valuable only when applied, and most effective when used consistently. The transformation you seek resides not in the mere acquisition of knowledge but in the application of it. It's about the choices you make each day, the patience you maintain with your progress, and the resilience you show in the face of life's complexities.

Reflect on your moments of awe, your newfound gratitude, and the peace you've cultivated as you've worked towards soothing your nervous system and freeing yourself from the constraints of a victim mindset. These are not transient experiences, but seeds planted within the fertile soil of your mind and soul, ready to grow with you.

However, be gentle with yourself. Change doesn't happen overnight. There will be days of struggle, confusion, and perhaps a sense of stagnation. These are as much a part of your journey as your successes and breakthroughs. Embrace them, learn from them, and let them guide your transformation.

As you step forward from this point, carry with you the understanding that you are the architect of your inner landscape. You have the power to construct a world that is grounded in mindfulness, nourished by gratitude, and resilient in the face of challenges.

So, dear reader, as you close this book, you're not concluding your journey. Instead, you're stepping into a new chapter of your life, armed with wisdom, inspired by hope, and guided by love. May your path forward be illuminated with clarity, enriched by purpose, and empowered by the unwavering belief in the extraordinary potential that resides within you.

Thank you for allowing this book to be a companion on your journey. May the journey ahead reveal even more profound layers of the magnificent, complex, and beautiful being that you are.

References & Resources:

Molecules of Emotion: Why You Feel the Way You Feel
Dr. Candace Pert

Becoming
By Michelle Obama

Atlas of the Heart: Mapping Meaningful Connection and the Language of Human Experience.
By Brené Brown

Awe: The Transformative Power of Everyday Wonder
By Professor Dacher Keltner

The Body Keeps the Score
By Dr. Bessel van der Kolk

Expressive Writing: Words That Heal
By Ph.D Pennebaker, James W. and John F. Evans

Breath
By James Nestor

Magnuson, C. D., & Barnett, L. A. (2013). "The playful advantage: How playfulness enhances coping with stress".

Proyer, R. T. (2013). "Playfulness and well-being in adults"

Guitard, P., Ferland, F., & Dutil, E. (2005). "Toward a better understanding of playfulness in adults"

Zhang, T. Y., & Li, H. (2014). "Play, exploration, and creativity: A literature review"

Play: How it Shapes the Brain, Opens the Imagination, and Invigorates the Soul
By Stuart Brown M.D. and Christopher Vaughan

A Secure Base
By John Bowlby

Patterns of Attachment: A Psychological Study of the Strange Situation
By Mary D. Salter Ainsworth

Yehuda, R., & Bierer, L. M. (2008). Transgenerational transmission of cortisol and PTSD risk. Progress in Brain Research, 167, 121-135. This paper examines how cortisol levels and PTSD symptoms may be passed from parents to their children, particularly in populations affected by severe trauma.

Yehuda, R., Schmeidler, J., Wainberg, M., Binder-Brynes, K., & Duvdevani, T. (1998). Vulnerability to posttraumatic stress disorder in adult offspring of Holocaust survivors. The American Journal of Psychiatry, 155(9), 1163-1171. This study explores the susceptibility to PTSD in the children of Holocaust survivors, suggesting a potential transgenerational transmission mechanism.

Yehuda, R., Engel, S. M., Brand, S. R., Seckl, J., Marcus, S. M., & Berkowitz, G. S. (2005). Transgenerational effects of posttraumatic stress disorder in babies of mothers exposed to the World Trade Center attacks during pregnancy. The Journal of Clinical Endocrinology & Metabolism, 90(7), 4115-4118. This research investigates the impact of maternal exposure to trauma (specifically, the 9/11 attacks) on their unborn children, indicating potential transgenerational effects.

Time with yourself is invaluable

Always enjoy it x